Wisdom Calls

Transformative Ways for Insightful Living

— HELEN WARWICK —

Sacristy
Press

Sacristy Press
PO Box 612, Durham, DH1 9HT

www.sacristy.co.uk

First published in 2023 by Sacristy Press, Durham

Scripture quotations, unless otherwise stated, are from the New Revised
Standard Version Bible: Anglicized Edition, copyright © 1989, 1995
National Council of the Churches of Christ in the United States of
America. Used by permission. All rights reserved worldwide.

Every reasonable effort has been made to trace the copyright holders
of material reproduced in this book, but if any have been inadvertently
overlooked the publisher would be glad to hear from them.

Sacristy Limited, registered in England & Wales, number 7565667

British Library Cataloguing-in-Publication Data
A catalogue record for the book is available from the British Library

ISBN 978-1-78959-313-6

I was a hidden treasure, and I loved to be known,
and so I created the worlds both visible and invisible.
Hadith Qudsi[1]

For the Community of Holy Rood House,
especially the guests who cultivate and enrich my own Wisdom
and that of the Community.

[1] Quoted in Cynthia Bourgeault, *The Wisdom Jesus: Transforming heart and mind—A new perspective on Christ and his message* (Boston, MA: Shambhala, 2008), p. 95.

Contents

Acknowledgements

I have been able to open to my own personal Wisdom through the support and encouragement of many people. I feel privileged to have heard and witnessed so many stories and experiences from everyone in the Holy Rood House Community, and I am most grateful for all the learning that we do together.

I had an experimental writing year encouraged by Kate Fox on a creative writing weekend at Holy Rood House. I am very grateful to Kate for this suggestion which helped me to explore and articulate Wisdom's ways.

I thank Elizabeth Baxter for her inspiration and encouragement to write.

June Boyce-Tillman has been most helpful in reading my manuscript and encouraging the book, and I really appreciate this support.

I have welcomed offers of writing spaces throughout the course of this book and thank Rosemary, Anne, Patti and Elizabeth for their generosity.

I am blessed to have wise and creative friends in my life, a special thank you to Anne, Hazel, Jane and Carla.

My lovely grandchildren Moira and Callum give me much delight, and I thank them for teaching me about innate Wisdom in such a joyful, imaginative way.

I realize that my father, Derek, has been travelling with me throughout this book. I have appreciated including his Wisdom within these pages and reflecting on the mysteries of after-life presence.

I include a heart-felt thank you to the Thirsk Quakers for their supportive presence in my life.

Paul Golightly and Capacitar UK teach me wonderful ways of wellbeing—I appreciate your dedication, Paul.

I am most grateful to Sacristy Press for believing in this book and getting it published.

My deep-felt thanks go to Nick who recognizes the head and heart space I need for writing. It is hard to express just how much your infinite love and support delights and enables me. I am truly grateful to have you journey with me.

Preface

Does not wisdom call,
and does not understanding raise her voice?
On the heights, beside the way,
at the crossroads she takes her stand;
beside the gates in front of the town,
at the entrance of the portals she cries out:
"To you, O people, I call,
and my cry is to all that live."

Proverbs 8:1–4

Wisdom speaks of the ancient path. We are connected to over three billion years of evolutionary Wisdom, starting from the earliest life forms. Symbols of Wisdom have been found dating from 3000 BC in the southwest of America in Native American rock art such as the arrow with a wavy line for the shaft, representing a person who is wise and true to themselves. In our current climate, Wisdom has come to represent many perspectives, connecting us to truth, to love, beauty, knowingness, and feeling more integrated.

This book has emerged through my own explorings of Wisdom within the therapeutic and educational community of Holy Rood House, Centre for Health and Pastoral Care. Our charity works on the margins of society, welcoming all, often guests who feel on the edge themselves, for short stay, day retreat and individual therapy. It is from this edge space that we listen for Wisdom's voice, emerging in a myriad of ways—assisted through stories, from the art room's creativity, and our earthy prayerfulness. My residential role as a Chaplain, Spiritual Director and Creative Therapist includes accompanying individuals, running retreats and offering wellbeing. An integral part for all staff is hospitality and it is within this nurturing welcome that Wisdom often emerges.

These are crucial times to hear the voice of Wisdom. Pandemics, wars and climate crisis are some of the instabilities reflected in the news, and there are always huge injustices that call for Wisdom's insight. In the early happenings of the coronavirus (Covid-19) pandemic, the online retreats I ran exploring Wisdom were among the most popular with our guests. There is a hunger for a way of being that is wise, that brings enlightenment and helps us discern the way through these difficult times. As we journey through the book, different perspectives of Wisdom will be explored that will open us to our own personal Wisdom and the relational connection to community and the earth. I am using a capital "W" for Wisdom throughout the book to accentuate the importance and authority that Wisdom carries, whatever perspective is being highlighted.

In the western world, we have been taught to favour logic and reason over the experiential ways of Wisdom. There will be strands of the scientific and rational included as evidence of some of Wisdom's aspects; however, Wisdom is not to be restricted; this poetic movement, evolving through energy within our bodies, is a flow and breath, bringing health and a way forward through our difficult paths. Personified as female in ancient sacred writings, she is steeped in everyday experience and ordinary life, emerging through our emotions and spirituality. Wisdom is difficult to articulate, and we may capture a flavour or scent of her from a space deeper than our thoughts. So the poems, stories, sayings, songs and prayers included throughout will help Wisdom breathe and enlarge. At the end of each chapter, there are creative ideas to develop our own Wisdom, with further explorations in the Appendices.

Using this book

As Wisdom comes through experience, I hope that readers will find their own Wisdom revelations throughout this book: a Wisdom that is personal and opens to a deeper presence. For Wisdom to emerge, we open to our curiosity as we read. We notice our feeling sense, and reflect on what is being brought forth. This alien way of reading requires a slowness, with that open awareness of what is being stirred within, perhaps with pen and paper to hand. Our reading might also need a discernment of what is right for our own Wisdom to emerge and what feels uncomfortable; there may be ideas that do not resound, or bring up conflicting thoughts. This is part of our curious stance; we always have a choice to accept or to disregard, and this is how our Wisdom comes forth.

Reading this book alongside a friend or using the material in a group will enhance our experience of Wisdom. As the thoughts offered are reflected upon and connected to our own personal experiences and stories, Wisdom will come forth, often with challenges that we can face with others and find a way through. It is in relationship that we learn to walk in the ways of Wisdom.

Introducing Wisdom

The Cry

Your cry has drawn me from my warm bed
Intriguing mixture of squawk and screech
A voice of one that sounds in the dark
That calls to be named

I am unprepared for this quest
My clothes lie hidden with one who sleeps
The open window allows greater sound
Placing you in the depths of the garden

Yet you, mysterious creature
Show me something to capture
A new voice, a sense of other
Here in this place
Drawing me out to the warm dark night[1]

Wisdom is elusive, wrapped in mystery. She can be humble, coming in the ordinary, in the now of the everyday moment, and she can surprise us with an epiphanic screech that draws us to follow her voice. Her call resounds within us, connecting us to our deepest longings and desires. Shadow-like, Wisdom draws us from darkness showing a way of healing, love, and care for ourselves and the earth. Her relational ways connect us to our deepest selves, and become a transformative voice bringing unity and belonging.

Certain disciplines and rhythms in life may coax her to emerge; she is worth hunting for, although she can't be forced. Wisdom is most apparent when adventuring on different trails from the normal, when getting lost and experiencing suffering. Here in our challenging times she enlarges and shows us her jewels. These jewels become treasures that can be shared in community as her stories inspire others.

Wisdom is an embodied presence—an innate aspect of our creation, central to our existence, that I refer to as "deep body-knowing". The psychoanalyst Carl Jung explored a source of Wisdom that is deep in all of our psyches. In listening to his clients and to himself, he noticed an "inner voice" that he attributed to a spiritual dimension. He noted Wisdom as an archetypal symbol, one grounded in our collective unconscious, inherited from our ancient ancestors. This Wisdom image may come to us through our dreams and our insights, and is one we will recognize in myths and legends where there is an old crone, or wise old man who will give guidance in the journey.

Dr Marsha Linehan, the developer of Dialectical Behaviour Therapy, believes that all people have within themselves the ability to be wise, using the phrase "wise mind" for this capacity for Wisdom. As a psychological concept, Wisdom holds the balance between the extremes of knowledge and doubt, of reason and emotion. Her balancing, relational ways connect us to our own explorings, especially as spiritual beings.

As Wisdom has a presence in all ancient cultures and all ancient faiths, I have had to open to my "wise mind" as to what to include in this book. The symbols of mythical creatures such as the two ravens Huginn and Muninn flying over the earth being the eyes and ears of Wisdom for the Norse god Odin, and the sacred figures such as Athena, the goddess of Wisdom, warfare and weaving in Greek mythology, give fascinating insights into Wisdom. I have honed my research on the many aspects of Wisdom to connect to the experience of myself and our community and, in regard to the spiritual, have mainly focused on Holy Wisdom— Hokhmah in the Hebrew and Sophia in the Greek. This research and articulation of Wisdom has been energizing and exciting and this is partly due to Wisdom's way of being a bridge between the ordinary and the spiritual.

Aristotle, the Greek philosopher born in 384 BC, sought after Sophia as that bridge between scientific knowledge and intuitive reason, *in seeking those things which are "highest by nature"*.[2] Holy Wisdom entices us across the bridge from our own body-knowing, to experience unique and varied aspects of her creative being, a few of which are expressed beautifully in the following verses.

The nature of Wisdom

There is in her a spirit that is intelligent, holy,
unique, manifold, subtle,
mobile, clear, unpolluted,
distinct, invulnerable, loving the good, keen,
irresistible, beneficent, humane,
steadfast, sure, free from anxiety,
all-powerful, overseeing all,
and penetrating through all spirits
that are intelligent, pure, and altogether subtle.[3]

Experiencing the bridge between logic and intuition, deep body-knowing and divinity, transpires through the creative process. This wonderful creative energy of Wisdom really comes to the fore in the creation myth described in Proverbs. She is introduced as being established by the Life behind all life as the creative presence to enable creation. This creative energy is key to exploring Wisdom as process:

From ages past, I am. I existed before the earth began.
I was there when the Being of beings made the
    blueprint for the earth and oceans.
I was the craftsperson, the weaver, at the side of Oneness.
I was the constant delight, rejoicing always in the
    presence of the Everlasting life-energy.[4]

As a "way" and as enlightenment, Wisdom is genderless. Hokhmah initiates the divine feminine, an aspect that has been hidden for many years and is an important voice for us today, especially in our patriarchal churches. The divine feminine has been worshipped in many ancient faiths, connecting to the bringing forth of life, of nurturing, creativity and the balance with the masculine. Terra-cotta figurines, with curvaceous breasts, around 15 cm tall, have been found in archaeological digs in the Holy Land. In Iron Age Judah, these figures were treasured in the Temple and in the home, reminding the people of this feminine aspect of God that gave life and held all things together in harmony. Thousands of these Judean pillar figures have been found, many shattered, as they were destroyed during reformations.[5]

Other reformations, especially under Roman occupation in the fourth century, also stifled Wisdom's voice. Under the influence of the Roman Emperor Constantine the Great, people were made to convert to Christianity, making faith a head-centred belief through the creeds, something one had to believe, rather than an experiential mystery people could open to. The first monastic communities moved away at this time and hid documents, many connected to the mystery of Hokhmah, not accepted by the Romans.

Some of these manuscripts have been uncovered over the years. In 1945, an Arab farmer digging for fertilizer, near the town of Nag Hammadi in Upper Egypt, came upon a metre-tall clay jar containing 13 leather-bound papyrus codices. Inside were 52 texts, including the Gospel of Thomas, the Gospel of Philip and Mary Magdalene, and the Secret Revelation of John. In *The Thunder, Perfect Mind*, written probably during the first pre-Christian century by an Alexandrian Jew, Wisdom manifests herself through a series of impressive paradoxes and themes, highlighting the tussles reflected within us:

> I was sent forth from the power,
> and I have come to those who reflect upon me,
> and I have been found among those who seek after me.

> For I am knowledge and ignorance.
> I am shame and boldness.
> Give heed to me.

I am she who exists in all fears
and strength in trembling.
I am she who is weak,
and I am well in a pleasant place.
I am senseless and I am wise.

I am the knowledge of my name.
I am the one who cries out,
and I listen.[6]

Hokhmah is referenced throughout these ancient hidden documents as well as in the mystical and philosophical books in the Bible and the Apocrypha, with a broad range of meaning, relating to divinity and the human. The writings included in the Bible were decided initially between the first and fourth century, with debates continuing until the sixteenth century. Although many of the Wisdom documents were not included, there are some such as Proverbs, Wisdom of Solomon and Song of Songs that were included, reflecting the Hebrews' love of Wisdom and her feminine ways. In the first century, beginning with the reign of Solomon, with his gifts of Wisdom and knowledge, Jewish thought had begun to concern itself with the great moral problems and mysteries of the world as well as the deep mysteries within themselves. These writings reflect the ancient Israelites' way of observing the world and human affairs as well as collating the experiences of past generations, opening a range of new and healing conceptions of God. The book of Job and some of the Psalms also reflect Wisdom's ways through the longing, suffering and questioning experienced.

Elizabeth Johnson writes of the relational aspects of Wisdom as Spirit-Sophia, Jesus-Sophia and Mother-Sophia; all of these connect to the transformational qualities of Wisdom.[7] As Spirit, Sophia connects to love and creativity, a movement that moves from within us, out to the Cosmos. As Mother, she brings forth life and is nurturer and earth connected. Jesus-Sophia highlights Christ as the Wisdom of God. Jesus followed the Wisdom tradition of the Israelites, drawing on the Jewish Wisdom tradition, and was a teacher of Wisdom. He lived and taught a way of transformation through parables and action, with his direct questioning, leading people to dig deeper within themselves.

Wisdom as a tradition connects to this ancient lineage of knowledge and practice found in faiths such as Buddhism, Christianity, the Jewish Kabbalah and Sufism. This tradition provides a framework for the development of the inner self and living a spiritual life with connection to the earth and divinity. There is emphasis on caring and sharing within community, within a greater power or Oneness. These principles will be included in the book following Wisdom in her divine and human nature.

As can be seen in this introduction, Wisdom enters into many "ologies"—psychology, theology, ecology, philosophy, anthropology, to name a few. In the following chapters, Wisdom will be explored in the ordinary, the earthed, through community and suffering, through writings and the voice of many, including our guests. Through this exploring we will find a Way—a truly transformational way that brings us to a unity and belonging with all of life.

Notes

[1]   Author, 2018, previously unpublished.

[2]   Celia Deane-Drummond, "Sophia: The Feminine Face of God as a Metaphor for an Ecotheology", *Feminist Theology* 16 (1997), pp. 11–31, quoting C. H. Chen, *Sophia: The Science Aristotle Sought* (Hildesheim: Georg Olms, 1976), p. 384.

[3]   Wisdom 7:22–3.

[4]   Rewriting from Proverbs 8:22–31.

[5]   To see images of these clay figures, put "Judean Pillar Figurines" into your search engine.

[6]   The Nag Hammadi Library, *The Thunder, Perfect Mind*, tr. George W. MacRae.

[7]   Elizabeth A. Johnson, *She Who Is: The Mystery of God in Feminist Theological Discourse* (New York: The Crossroad Publishing Company, 1998).

CHAPTER 1

Wisdom calls through the body

Two kinds of intelligence

There are two kinds of intelligence.
One is like that acquired by a child at school
from books and teachers, new ideas and memorization.
... the other kind of intelligence is a gift
its fountain is deep within

it flows continually from the house of the heart.
Seek the fountain within yourself.[1]

As Rumi, a thirteenth-century Persian poet and Sufi master, shows us, the concept of a knowing within the body that is fresh and continually flowing is very different from intelligence. This concept of Wisdom that is situated deep within the body is informed from our ancient ancestors who concerned themselves with transforming ways and founded listening practices. Wisdom is not about knowing more; it is about knowing more deeply.

Our post-Enlightenment western culture prefers reason and problem-solving rather than listening to the body with its intuitive ways, as there is still much suspicion around the intuitive, emotional and spiritual, which are all areas linked to Wisdom.

For about seven years in the early noughties, I lived with chronic illness—ME or Chronic Fatigue Syndrome. Within this very disabling condition, I tried to find out what my body was telling me. As the body's language is non-verbal, I needed to find ways of observing, listening and connecting to the body, so its messages could be revealed. Since this time,

I have found ways of opening to my deep body-knowing—the way the body can lead us on our healing path.

In the present moment, the body tells it as it is; it cannot lie; hence our body is a sign of our true nature. As we find ways of listening and reflection (and these ways will differ as we are so unique), we will open to the Wisdom of the body. This is a place of deep truth, of hope, of knowing the next step connecting to life and love. It is easy to be shut off from this deep place within, made more difficult by the fact that it is not talked about, taught or acknowledged in our western society. We are also used to wanting others to sort out whatever is happening in our bodies. We turn to the doctors and the people we might suppose are wiser than ourselves.

Within our community of Holy Rood House, we work with the connection to our bodies, being aware of how anxiety and stress, trauma and abuse, can shut us off from our bodies. Many are repulsed by their body, and we need to tread carefully with finding ways to gently introduce a relationship with the body. Our bodies have ways of defending and protecting ourselves in traumatic times and this often requires armour plating to keep us going. We might find ways to dissociate when images or memories are remembered, taking us out of the body and the pain of the emotions. Self-harm sometimes happens through feeling numb and being unable to connect to our "self". Self-inflicted pain might help to feel something rather than nothing. We have to be nurturing to our bodies, to allow our bodies to do what is right at the time. Some guests say to me that they don't even think about their bodies—it is just something they live in unawares. As a community, we try and find the nurturing voice, connected to love, that will enable this relationship with our body. My hope is that those who may struggle with this chapter will find gentle encouragement and feasible small ways to bring about a healthier relationship with their body.

There is often a tussle between our intellect and our intuition, a long gap between head and heart or head and gut. The term "wise mind" is used by Dr Marsha Linehan to describe the place where reasonable mind and emotional mind overlap. The reasonable mind is the part of the mind that is rational, that makes decisions and analyses facts. The emotional mind makes decisions on how we feel. This more unpredictable mind can go through instabilities with the sway of heightened emotions, making us doubt and mistrust our body at times. The integration of the reasonable mind and the emotional mind is the wise mind—bringing the observance of our feelings to our rational thought, especially useful for making our decisions:

> Wise mind is that part of each person that can know and experience truth. It is where the person knows something to be true or valid. It is almost always quiet; it has a certain peace. It is where the person knows something in a centered way.[2]

I was offering a creative exercise on the wise mind with some guests in our art room. The rational and emotional minds were drawn out as two circles with an overlap in the middle for the wise mind, creating spaces to write or draw about each. One guest said she would like to have a third circle—the recuperating mind. There are times when we don't want to activate decisions or connect to our Wisdom, and perhaps this sense of recuperation can be a motivator to explore these different aspects.

It is only relatively recently that the Wisdom of the body has been explored by biochemists in modern medicine through the action of chemical transmitters, called neuropeptides, which transmit impulses along the nerves. Dr Candace Pert, who has researched into the role of neuropeptides, emotions and the immune system, refers to the "bodymind"—the mind and body working as an integrated whole, because at the level of the neurotransmitter there is no separation between the mind and the body. The neurotransmitters were originally thought to be only in the brain, but now they have been found in internal organs, especially the gut, heart and immune system. So there is a way for messages to be initiated and transmitted through our organs as well as the brain. For example, our gut has the same peptides and receptors as those found in the brain. The web of nerves found in this area is second in complexity to the human brain, and the richness and diversity of the receptors may be why a lot of people feel their emotions in their gut, an important aspect of intuition.[3]

Neuropeptides are produced by nerve cells and when they lock into their receptors, which are attached to other cells in the body, they make something happen (or prevent it from happening). The receptors the neuropeptides lock on to enable the information exchange of the different functions of the central nervous system, including sleep, arousal, pain, cognition, stress responses, and emotions. Night and day each cell in our body is negotiating with the organ it is part of, and that organ with its organ system, and that organ system with the whole body.

Neuropeptides represent an ancient and widespread mode of neuronal communication. They have been found in identical formulations in *all* forms of life. Even the simplest of protozoa makes the same neuropeptides as we do. The molecule for one of the rat's brain receptors is very similar to one of our brain receptors, and I find this amazing that the way our bodies make messages is with the same materials for all life. These chemical transmitters may provide a molecular basis for communication between all living species, messages of which we are largely unaware. Who knows the ripple effect of our meditation, prayer and our thinking of others?

The mind has the ability to choose and is the conscious self. The body reacts without choice, hence subconsciously. Through this subconscious process our bodies react to all that is going on. This is why we need to have a nurturing voice with our body, as it will be reacting to many aspects that have accumulated through our lives. This is a difficult process to observe, and yet, to have connection to the body it is interesting to note what brings reaction in our bodies. What stirs our emotions, what causes pain, what nudges us to drink and eat? All of us already access our own Wisdom—we often don't pause and acknowledge this. How do we actually get through our day from the time we awaken in the morning to making the decision to take our bodies to bed at night?

To become aware of sensations in our body we need a sense of stilling or quietening, to allow that listening. Connecting to our breath can be helpful, something that we do automatically, and when focused on intentionally can bring us into awareness of our body. We may then become aware of the subtle sounds and sensations—heart beats, gurglings, swallowing, blinking that goes on all the time. As we bring our awareness to our sensations and senses, we can get in touch with a deeper sense, a sacred sense. This has various names and is found in many religions. "Sixth sense" or intuition is a way of knowing something we cannot know rationally. In religious paintings of many cultures, a light often shines around the point of the Third Eye, between the eyebrows—known as the centre of intuition and the eye of consciousness in the Hindu and Buddhist faiths.

Holy Wisdom or Hokhmah or Sophia, found in ancient Hebrew and Greek manuscripts, is named as the breath of Life or the wise breath of interiority, and it is only through our senses and sensations (not words or concepts) that we connect to this "sacred sense". Through Hokhmah, we become aware of "one who senses", a greater presence within, which will be explored further throughout the book, and could be termed the "knower" within us:

> When we confront the "knower" within us, the one that experiences, we enter the presence of what these storytellers call Hokhmah, Holy Wisdom or the "sacred sense." From the meaning of her name, she is "the breath of awareness from underneath and within."[4]

When we are connecting to what we can feel, hear, smell, taste and touch we are acknowledging what is going on in our bodies. We cannot be ruminating on thoughts when we are listening to the birds, feeling the temperature of the air on our skin or smelling a lovely aroma. Within the wellbeing practices that I organize, when we are focusing on the senses, I always leave the visual sense until last as it is often through the visual that we may get too much stimulation. In this practice, we use a gentle gaze, to see what the body notices. There may be a colour, shape, or object that we are drawn to. Noticing what we are drawn to means that the "focused on" may impart something for us that is needed in that moment—maybe a colour or beauty that uplifts us, reminding us of something that is helpful.

For people who have one or more of their senses affected, often the remaining senses improve. We had a masseur contributing in our community for years who had limited sight and perhaps a more intuitive sense of touch. He was also great at DIY! There is a lovely phrase of Shakespeare's when King Lear asks the blind man Gloucester "How do you see the world?", and Gloucester replies "I see it feelingly."[5]

For all of us, increasing our awareness of our senses will bring us into the present moment and allow us that gentle way to our body-knowing:

> I am a sensual being and as I notice my emotions, enjoy the way
> my tongue moves on my lower lip, relish the smell of lavender,
> I become aware of the one who Senses. I can only do this as I
> relax, become vulnerable and learn to trust this process and let
> this lead to my trusting centre. As I do this the Senser comes to
> life, unencumbered by anxiety and stress.[6]

We can have this connection to our bodies throughout the day. Whatever
we do we are sensing. Acknowledging the body as we brush our teeth,
queue in the shop, get ready for bed, gives chance for our intuition
to arise in those present moments. Observing our own non-verbal
expressions can also inform. The way we use our hands in speech, ruffle
our hair, soothe our skin. When I speak to a group, I try and keep my
body language in check as sometimes our bodies want to stretch or be
soothed, especially if we are nervous. On one occasion, as I was speaking
to a group of people, I became aware of my left leg hovering horizontal
to the ground, and I slowly eased it down whilst I talked!

At Holy Rood House, we encourage various ways of connection to
our bodies. The gardens offer spaces to engage with our senses. Our
resident gardener often spends time with guests, highlighting the plants
and wildlife. I took a highly anxious person, who was in a lot of pain,
out into the garden to pick flowers, which really helped her to appreciate
the flowers and forget her issues. We have many events in the garden,
including circle dancing, wellbeing practices and prayer times.

Our Chapel spaces offer possibilities for the meeting of the rational
and intuitive through prayer and the Eucharist. Our regular prayer times
in the Chapel offer pauses to connect to our breath and inclusion of
liturgy where the body is highlighted as the earthing of our spirit, as a
holder of our sacred sense.

One of the suggestions I make to guests who want to explore more
of the body connection is to go into one of our larger rooms in Juliet
House, called the Drama room, put a "Do not Disturb" on the door, and
use the space to let the body lead: to move, to dance, to curl up in a foetal
position, whatever the body wants to do. Often the body takes us through
a process that gives us clues or "sorts us out" in a way that feels right; it
somehow expresses the inexpressible. One guest, who had a degenerative

condition affecting her eyesight, took up this idea. She found a static start led her to begin flowing and moving with a sense of freedom and flying. A very physical person, she took her experience to the art room, using energetic strokes and colours to depict dancing figures. The experience connected to her energy and sense of play and childlikeness. It helped her with the grief for her many losses from her restrictions.

I love to dance with her

The gentle rhythm of your breath
The cold earth solid beneath my feet
The warm sun resting on my shoulders.

Life fills my being
The beauty, the fascination, the intimacy of Her creation moves
My soul
And my spirit dances within me.

My body is mine
It's aching
It's beautiful curves
It's stretching
It's curling into itself
It's asleep and it's waking.

It lives and pulsates life and creativity
Anger and despair
Hope and passion.

It is my body
I love to dance with her in
The changing seasons
The dawning of spring through to the drab colours of winter
Of coldness and death
All are yours and all are mine
It is the celebration of life
It is the dance of salvation the rhythm of healing.[7]

Our intuition is always ahead of our conscious—so we can get a sense of something before it happens, or an increased understanding. We often *know* when something is wrong; we get a feeling, perhaps in our guts: new mothers intuit much about their new-born babies at a time when they may feel overwhelmed, and we often have a knowing when someone is lying to us or deceiving us in some way as we read the face of others in so many unconscious ways. Bringing our intuition to consciousness, allowing reflection with the rational mind, helps us to name these fleeting feelings and gives us courage to follow more of the prompts of our intuition.

Our intuition may also prepare ourselves before something major happens. Our bodies have this knowing that can lead us to talk to someone, read something, visit somewhere that helps with future events. One guest decided to read a book over a year with 52 brain-training exercises to protect against stress and help with resilience. At the end of the year, she had a huge shock to her life and felt that somehow she had been led to prepare for this unexpected crisis.

It is often when we are not using logical ways and thinking hard, when we are in the present moment, connecting to our senses, that our intuition is able to surface. This intuitive place within opens out with slow, relaxed ways. The brain has different speeds of wave patterns for various functions. The high arousal state that our brains are often in— being stimulated through TV, phone and computer screens and emotions such as anxiety and fear—keeps us from accessing our Wisdom which needs the slower brain waves of the alpha wave pattern.[8] This is the more relaxing state, one where we slow down, connect to the present, walk in nature and perhaps create with our hands. When we connect to our breath, and breathe slower and deeper, our brain waves slow to a different function, one that allows us to feel more integrated as the alpha wave pattern opens a wider area of the brain and frees access to our emotions and imagination. We can be more creative in the alpha state and healing is able to take place with this connection with body and mind. It is important to note that Wisdom *frees up* our minds—we open out to Wisdom, and this releases energy and connects us to a spaciousness, whereas knowledge is accumulative and the logical mind stimulates.

Wisdom takes us to a deeper place within, a sacred space under the clutter of everyday woes and chaos. Dr Linehan describes the wise mind like a deep well in the ground, the water at the bottom of the well linking to the entire underground ocean of the wise mind.[9] Wisdom as an underground spring or river, as mentioned by the Rumi poem at the start of the chapter, connects to a vastness, a freeing spaciousness. Many of our guests who feel restricted, smothered or shut down in some way, find the possibility of having space within, to explore, dance and uncover our Wisdom, a revolutionary thought. We often run our lives from the everyday occurrences and what is going on in our heads. This spacious, deeper place is always there, reflecting the stability, peace and Wisdom we can obtain.

For Etty Hillesum, a Dutch Jew, this spaciousness within enabled her to get through huge suffering. She explored her life through copious journaling in the last two years of her life, during the Second World War. She kept her inner life alive amidst this terrible time of suffering and appreciated the help she got from a Jungian analyst.

> That spatial feeling within me is very strong ... As if infinite steppes lay spread out inside me—I can see them and feel them and move over them. That one should carry such an awe-inspiring space within oneself. The inner world is as real as the outer world ... It too has landscapes, contours, possibilities, its boundless regions.[10]

Within this spaciousness she found what was deepest and best within her, which she called "God". She reflected and faced many issues through this inner landscape. She had suffered from depression throughout her life, but she found that connecting to this inner landscape paved the way to uplift her, to connect her to hope and gladness.

This sense of inner space can be really helpful to our squashed selves, with its knowing giving us a sense of accompaniment. Many of our guests who feel incredibly alone have been helped by this concept of Wisdom as an accompanier, as one who guides, one who is within us, carried around wherever we go. Once we are more open to Wisdom's voice, she will help in the care we need to nurture our bodies. We will become more confident in what our bodies need to eat, for resting, and to say no to what is not right for us.

Our bodies go through various rhythms throughout the day and many seasons during our lifetime. For women, menstruation, ovulation, pregnancy, childbirth, perimenopause and menopause, are intense physical and psychological experiences that offer us a grounding in our body Wisdom. From ancient cultures, religions and mythologies, the concept of the Triple Goddess highlights three important areas of development in women—the Maiden, the Mother and the Crone. These aspects, the Maiden being the child, enjoying play and the anticipation of life, the Mother the loving nurturer with the ability to give birth (to our endeavours and creative pursuits) and the wise Crone, are also aspects of ourselves—male or female. The Crone represents the Wisdom that comes with age and experience, as well as the ability to deal with further mysteries such as death and darkness. She is the wise woman that can pass her Wisdom on to others, being an encourager and healer.

The psychologist Erikson, who defined eight stages of human development, had the last stage of life corresponding to the Crone abilities. He believed that any development missed earlier can be made up later, so the latter years of our lives can be important as reflection, healing and processing times.[11]

The varying energies that come through all these stages (which will be explored further in the next chapter) encourage our development of intuition: from the curiosity and sensuousness of the Maiden, through the giving and receiving of the Mother, to the connection to the energy from the spiritual nature of the Crone. As our energy changes through all the seasons in our lives, so we are opened to different aspects of gaining intuition.

Ideas to connect to our body Wisdom

Senses and breath

Getting connected to our senses and our breath helps us to centre down and link to the observer within. Breathing in and out, perhaps slower and deeper, helps us connect directly with our bodies, getting out of our head space. Our senses—especially touch or feeling, hearing and smell—help us to open to our body awareness.

Observing the body, its sensations, its habits, the way it moves and articulates

To be able to observe ourselves we imagine taking a step away from all that is going on in our heads and emotions. This can be hard to do at first, and sometimes the image of looking at ourselves as in a camera or facing ourselves in a mirror may be helpful. For those who struggle with connecting to the body, a beginning might be to talk through this observing with a trusted, loving other. The observer of ourselves needs to be non-judgemental, just noticing how the body is reacting, what stirs our emotions and how our energy lifts and sinks. Each reaction is seen with an intrigue, an interest, rather than an involvement or judgement. Our body is what it is; we are the noticer of the body doing what it needs to do.

If we are able to still ourselves, we can observe the sensations of the body, the pulses, gurgles, thoughts, eye blinks and breathing for instance. As we observe the body, we connect to "that which senses", the Wisdom of the body as the Senser.

Observing the mind and the voice/s that drive us

It can be very interesting noticing what is going on in our heads, what thoughts, images and sounds might be floating around. It is difficult for our minds to be clear and still, so we often have a continual stream of narration and images. Our thoughts often link to an inner voice that is the narrator for our thoughts. Sometimes this voice is critical—many of us are harsh on ourselves—with thoughts that include needing to do things right, going over past difficulties, and judging our actions. Once we notice what is going on in our thoughts, what images occur, any songs or patterns, we can start to manage them. We have a choice as to what goes on in our minds. We can notice these observations as a surface narration, and then pause and imagine connecting to a deeper spaciousness, perhaps a deep well within. Here we open to Wisdom and the freedom to notice what is restricting us and what is giving us life. We may choose not to focus on the hurtful thoughts, we may focus on the smaller things that are happening, or the song in our head that might have meaning to our present lives—either for its pace, lyrics or melody:

> Step aside from all thinking,
> and there is nowhere you can't go.
> Returning to the root, you find the meaning.[12]

Bringing in the nurturing voice

It is harder for us to connect to our Wisdom if we do not value our bodies and trust that we do have something innate that will be of help to us. It is especially difficult for those who have not had good nurturing in the early years of their lives, or struggle to trust as a result of traumatic experiences.

We can imagine a nurturing voice within, perhaps what a good friend would say, or a respected wise person. The nurturing voice is connected to love and is often hidden and hard to find. Hearing what the voice of love would say, or encourage, can often bring another perspective into our lives that leads us on a more healing path. Once captured, this voice needs to have the volume turned up, to allow it to be heard over the critical voice within us.

One of the ways of affirming our intuition is through kindness. We can bring in more nurturing for our body—a bit of pampering, relaxing, soothing and finding a way of touch for our bodies that is helpful and calming.

Listen and reflect

To connect to the body, times of active listening, of opening our inner ears, being aware of what is going on in and around us, but not getting absorbed or distracted by this, can be helpful. It is an alert listening of just noting what is and can bring us to a stillness where Wisdom is able to surface. Perhaps a thought comes up, an idea, that feels like it comes from a different space to the head. This is another way of going deeper into that reflective watery space within.

Reflection enriches the listening experience. Within a quiet space, having times of reflecting on what has happened in our day, our week, we can realize what is important to us and our connections. Wisdom comes from experience that is reflected upon.

We may need some experiment to know how best to put aside these times. Switching off mobile phones and coming away from distractions can help. For those who find sitting still difficult, listening through walking, swimming, the quiet stilling of a craft or colouring may help.

Finding what the body wants

We can ask what our bodies need and try and listen to the answers. We could do this by having times of moving and stretching, letting the body lead in a private space, or perhaps we could have a walk outside letting the body take us where it wants to go. We may prefer to write—using two colours, one for asking the questions as ourselves, and the other with answering the questions as "our body".

In these spaces, we need to note the season our bodies are going through. Is it a particularly stressful time in our lives? Maybe we are going through a change—within the body, or in our circumstances. We take into account all that is going on for us in the present.

What is the right rhythm for our bodies that will be a healthy way for us? What are the best times of day for waking up, going to bed, having the best energy?[13]

Finding the right practices for connecting to our bodies

We will all have our own unique preferences for exercise and what appeals, to find a way of better connection to our bodies. Walking, cycling, yoga, tai chi, group games, jogging: there is a vast wealth of ways. Body therapies, such as massage, are an important aspect of Holy Rood House, taking into account the gentleness needed for some to be introduced to a connection to their bodies.

Capacitar (which means to awaken and encourage) is an international organization teaching body-based practices that empower people to access their inner Wisdom to heal and transform themselves, and their communities. They offer many helpful practices found online, from acupressure, meditation and body holds that are for all ages.[14]

Creative ideas for this chapter

An exercise for opening to Wisdom of the body

We settle ourselves in a comfortable position bringing into awareness our breathing, breathing in and breathing out, slowing and deepening our breathing over a few minutes. We try and bat away any distracting thoughts, knowing that thoughts will always come in these times and allowing them to drift away without engaging with them. We may note the feel of the chair on our body, the temperature of the air on our skin, any tensions we have in the body. We can breathe into any pain or tension and notice when breathing out for any release.

We connect to our hearing and imagine a sense of inner hearing. We listen to any body sensations—gurgles and buzzes. We open up a sense of an inner eye, a visual imagining of a channel or pathway to our inner Wisdom.

So we breathe and listen; we breathe and notice.

We may like to continue to imagine Wisdom as deep flow within, perhaps a spring connecting to an underground river, or a well connecting to the bedrock of the earth. We imagine this spaciousness within us and the gift this can be.

We take time for these imaginings, giving space afterwards to write or draw any glimpses that are helpful.

An exercise to hear our inner Wisdom

We begin with the breath, batting away distractions and focusing on breathing in and out. When we feel settled, we imagine going down a path. We don't think too hard about this; we let a path emerge. As we go down this path, we see a building of some kind. We may go into this building where we imagine meeting a wise person. This may be a character we know or one we imagine. What will this wise person look like? What might they be doing? We imagine a conversation with this wise person, taking time to be with this character. We may make some notes or draw an image from this meeting.

We might prefer to write out some words that a wise person might say. A development could be to have a two-colour felt-tip conversation. One colour is ourselves; we may like to ask questions and listen to the answers of the wise person, written in the other colour.

A prayer for Wisdom

Deep within us God is holy
Wisdom planted in the dark
We are dreaming, searching slowly
Softly will our journey start

Deep within a seed is growing
Petals form the flower head
Beauty lights the path that's flowing
Through the dried-up riverbed

In the shimmering we are listening
To the fruitful voice within
In our waiting, in our glistening
Truthful living can key in[15]

Notes

[1] Tehreem Fatima Sabir <https://tehreemfatima.weebly.com/>. <https://allpoetry.com/Two-Kinds-of-Intelligence> for another version of this poem.

[2] Dr Marsha Linehan <https://www.dbtselfhelp.com/html/wise_mind.html>.

[3] Kat Duff, *The Alchemy of Illness* (New York: Pantheon, 1993), pp. 108–9. <http://candacepert.com/articles/the-wisdom-of-the-receptors-neuropeptides-the-emotions-and-the-bodymind/>.

[4]   Neil Douglas-Klotz, *Desert Wisdom: A Nomad's Guide to Life's Big Questions from the Heart of the Native Middle East* (Worthington: ARC Books, 2011), p. 87.

[5]   Shakespeare, *King Lear* Act 4, Scene 6, Line 164.

[6]   From my personal journaling.

[7]   Guest at Holy Rood House, 2000, *Poetry and Art from Holy Rood House: A Celebration of 25 Years 1993–2018* (independently published, 2019), p. 167.

[8]   For more information on alpha waves and tips on increasing alpha state: <https://www.verywellmind.com/what-are-alpha-brain-waves-5113721>.

[9]   Dr Marsha Linehan <https://dbtselfhelp.com/dbt-skills-list/mindfulness/wise-mind/>.

[10] Etty Hillesum, *Etty: The Letters and Diaries of Etty Hillesum 1941–1943*, ed. Klaus A. D. Smelik, tr. Arnold J. Pomerans (Grand Rapids, MI: Eerdmans Publishing Co., 2002), pp. 60, 204, 435.

[11] For Eric Erikson's Stages of Psychosocial Development, see Matthew Linn, Sheila Fabricant and Dennis Linn, *Healing the Eight Stages of Life* (New York: Paulist Press, 1988) and also <http://psychology.about.com/od/psychosocialtheories/a/psychosocial.htm>.

[12] Seng-Ts'an (?—606), Chinese Zen Master; from Stephen Mitchell (ed.), *The Enlightened Heart: An Anthology of Sacred Poetry* (New York: HarperCollins, 1994).

[13] Further explanations and exercises for observing and understanding the body can be found in my book *The Life-giving Path* (New Town Farm: Kevin Mayhew, 2016), especially in the Personal Room, the Spacious Room and the Library.

[14] <https://capacitar.org/>.

[15] June Boyce-Tillman, "Deep within us God is holy", *A Rainbow to Heaven* (London: Stainer & Bell, 2006), p. 22. © 2006 Stainer & Bell Ltd, 23 Gruneisen Road, London N3 1LS, www.stainer.co.uk. Used by permission. All rights reserved.

CHAPTER 2

Wisdom calls through process

As our path unfolds, we continually give birth to ourselves since, as our life changes, we discover new ways of being and knowing.[1]

In the last chapter, we explored a connection to Wisdom through our senses and our self-observations. We can open to a spaciousness within. This chapter explores how we become aware of Wisdom emerging—the process of this emerging. It is through our ordinary lives that we can explore this process of transformation that leads us to deeper insight, to feeling more connected to ourselves and the world around us.

Wisdom as process is hard to articulate. I recall the art exhibition where the abstract artist had started her canvas with colourful intricate forms and then covered most of these forms in thick monochrome paint leaving tantalizing small windows. Wisdom is about sensing the not seen. We often catch glimpses of feelings, images, energy, words and thoughts that enlighten us.

Wisdom is a way, a process, a movement that is transformational. Genesis, the first book of the Bible with the story of the unfolding of the universe, means coming into being or "becoming" in Greek. Wisdom process is a movement of becoming, of emerging and new beginnings. We transform, alongside the earth. The characteristic of Wisdom process is often mystery—it is not clearly voiced. This sense of mystery is important as it challenges our rational nature.

I am offering a cautionary note at the beginning of this chapter, because elements in it may evoke great resistance. Opening to Wisdom requires an awakening—an awakening to what is going on, especially within ourselves and in our lives. Hildegard of Bingen, the twelfth-century Benedictine abbess and visionary, wrote that to become wise is to be "aroused for living".[2] Many of us prefer to slumber, for various reasons, often connected to pain, fear and the busyness of life. We prefer not to stop, not to notice, because what might we feel, what might we find? Both pausing and noticing are skills that can open Wisdom's ways. This is why I will take us gently through this chapter, so that we may find the right pace and nurturing for ourselves and find confident ways to connect to Wisdom; for she will guide us to a store of energy, intuition and healing.

To initiate the process of becoming we begin with noticing what is going on in our own body. In the last chapter, we considered the observer stance, and in this way of perceiving we notice our own processes connected to our energies, emotions and thoughts. Noticing can be a very alien way of working for us; it was certainly a tool that took me a while to establish, so I will start with how we learn to notice, continue with what we are noticing and summarize with how we can encourage this noticing.

Some steps for noticing

Noticing through the power of the pause

To be able to notice what is going on we need to be able to pause, to stop. This can be transformational in itself as we bring into our day pauses where we come into the present moment and notice our outer and inner environments. Pausing also offers us time to choose whether we want to continue in our day in the state of mood and mind we register. As we pause and notice, we create space for choice as to how we want to continue. On my notice board, I have a quote by Victor Frankl which reads: "Between stimulus and response there is a space and in that space lies our power to choose."

We can pause at intervals in our day, and at any time when we feel our emotions stirred or a shift in our energies. I appreciate poetry with its way of articulating something of the small happenings in my day, or the deeper happenings in my interior journey. As I read a poem, a line or verse might resonate and stir a feeling, memory or sensation within me. This is where I try and pause and notice, letting those lines reveal an inner epiphany.

Noticing through connecting to our breath

Wisdom is a movement, an energy, an emerging from our unconscious and our breath connects us to this movement. This is wonderfully explained through the Hebrew word *nephesh*, which translates in various ways, the roots of the word connecting to breath. Neil Douglas-Klotz, a world-renowned scholar in religious studies, spirituality and psychology, describes *nephesh*, from the Native Middle Eastern tradition, as the seed-self, or soul-self within us.[3] This has a three-part nature with the inspiring in-breath and the reaction to that inspiration causing a sense of expansion within, that then moves outwards; the movement of the out-breath generates motivation and gives us life. Each living creature is a *nephesh*, a living being, and through our breath we are connected to all life.

Noticing through imagining a spaciousness within

In the western world we are often logical, head-space people. Noticing comes from a deeper place, a spaciousness introduced in the last chapter, sometimes termed a heart space, where the body releases its intuitive nature.

As we learn to come into this spaciousness to notice (and there will be an exercise at the end to aid this movement), we can take courage in what this depth offers, a tuning in to aspects that our logical mind cannot compute—aspects such as love, truth, beauty and joy. The movement of Wisdom opens us to these aspects through our emotions and senses, rather than through our logic. In this spaciousness, oneness and wholeness are perceived, a sense of unity with others and the earth.

Meister Eckhart, a thirteenth- and fourteenth-century German medieval theologian, philosopher and mystic, researched this spaciousness, calling it "soul", which is not a definable place or a noun, but a movement in Compassion and Love.[4]

During the writing of this chapter, I had a dream: I travelled to a clear lake; still waters that I knew were sacred and where other people gathered. I knew I had to remove most of my clothes, get into the water, and let go, to let myself sink to the sandy bottom of this lake, to sit on the bottom and then rise. There was something of a ritual about this and I did this, slowly, a few times. I had a calmness about me, a sense of doing what was right to do.

I have had other dreams of being under water, and having to hold my breath, not being sure whether I can make it to the bottom and rise to the surface. In this present dream, breathing was not an issue. The dream spoke to me of letting go, of taking off outer garments or things that restrict and to trust the going under the water, where, in this spaciousness we learn that we too can breathe.

Noticing through the creative process

As we open to our deeper body-knowing we open out, through our *nephesh*, to inspiration and ideas. We have this opportunity throughout the day as we may pause to notice how we chose the clothes to wear that day, the food to prepare, what music to hear and ideas that emerge. We encourage guests to use the art room at Holy Rood House. Those guests who say they are not creative and expect not to be able to manage any creative activity, often connect to the creative way of Wisdom process; this can be less true of those who come with a preconceived idea of what they want to produce or an expectation of creative skill. Outcome is less important than the creative process itself, in which we need to let the body lead. In play and exploration, using our hands, getting messy with paint or clay, tearing out pictures from magazines, we encourage our creativity that guides our path.

This is a way for ideas to birth, drawing us into our becoming. It is worth noting that it is often from our depths that ideas bubble up, rather than focusing on the higher functions of our minds by thinking really hard and trying to focus on problem-solving. It is often when we stop, get into our senses, into the present moment, we get a way to move to the next moment. We "know" what to do in that next moment.

On the first day of a weaving retreat, guests were encouraged to choose one or two colours of wool and a piece of loose-weave fabric and start to stitch or weave in and out, in whatever way they wished. Some had never done any weaving or stitching before, and we reviewed at the end of the session how they came to produce what they did: what led them to the colour and activated what they produced? At the end of the weekend, one woman commented that she appreciated the trust that I had, at that very first session, that they would all have the ability to produce some weaving. I stated that I knew that everyone has this activating, creative way within them. I know it within myself and have seen it so many times with guests; this is particularly true of guests who say they are not creative, in whom, after connecting with the textures, colours and materials, transformation happens.

The following is a poem about this creative process, speaking as creative spirit.

Creative Spirit

You feel me flutter in the deep
eager to emerge
My gestation needs patience
disciplines of eye, ear, stitch and still
It is my urge, driver to your journey
to play, explore, notice

On your rising
I quiver and enlarge
I am midwife
release, flow
I require presence,

vulnerability
sense of trust
inquisitive openness

I connect you
to belonging
Feel the earth
ground your feet
laugh[5]

What are we noticing?

Noticing what attracts us

As we go through our day, we can use the "pause" to notice what attracts us. If we all went as a group to a place to look around, we would all notice different objects, colours, shapes and happenings. That is because we are all unique and what attracts one of us will bypass another. Noticing what attracts us feeds into who we are as a unique human being; this is so important as we find ways to connect to Wisdom's movement that reveals our identity. As we appreciate more of what attracts us—what colour we are drawn to, which tree fascinates, a spoken word—we find out more about ourselves and move in the direction of what is right for us, boosting our self-esteem.

In our airy art room at Holy Rood House, we encourage guests to go with what they notice and to experiment and explore. One example (and I could give many) is of a woman in her seventies who came to one of our creative days. She was attracted to the clay, and once set up, she played around with this tactile material for a while. She then found a poem bubbled up from somewhere—all about her husband, who had died ten years earlier. The exploring with her hands had taken her out of her head space, into the leadings of her body. She had never written a poem before and wanted the group to hear the poem when we were in the Chapel space later in the day. We were all able to connect to the man she had known for so many years, to witness the love, and encourage her in her exploring.

Sapientia is Latin for Wisdom, which is derived from the verb *sapere*—to taste and savour something, giving us another aspect of Wisdom which is the ability to savour life. As we notice what attracts us, what we are drawn to, we pause to savour, and taste the delights that are offered in our lives. It is often in the brief happenings and sightings in our day—the food we taste, a beauty that captivates, a smell, a texture, a smile—where we can pause and savour, and open to Wisdom's way.

Noticing our energy

Hokhmah, Holy Wisdom, has many descriptions connecting to life and energy, such as breath of Life and the symbol of the Tree of Life. Coming into being as energy in the myth of creation, through the Everlasting life-energy, she reflects our life-force, our creative life spark, that is key to our breathing and our beating heart. This life-force energy is recognized through many cultures and called by many names such as Chi, Qi, Prana and Christ life. This energy is our "aliveness" described beautifully by Cynthia Bourgeault:

> Each one of us and each action we take has a quality of aliveness—an inner aliveness—a fragrance or vibrancy uniquely its own. If the outer form of who we are in this life is conveyed by our physical bodies, the inner form—our real beauty and authenticity—is conveyed in the quality of our aliveness. This is where the secret of our being lies. Quality is the innermost, energetic essence of our own life, shining through the outer skin of our being.[6]

We hear many stories of people surviving in extreme circumstances and hanging on to life through connection to love: this life-force energy is pure energy that makes up who and what we are. Scientists have now discovered that all matter in the universe is fundamentally made up of energy—something that the writers of the book of Wisdom knew in mid-first century BC:

> For wisdom is more mobile than any motion;
> because of her pureness she pervades and penetrates all things.[7]

In the Kabbalah—the Jewish mystical literature—one system shows the first divine emanation as nothingness, with Hokhmah as the point between nothingness and being; this connects with images such as the seed in the womb or the source of the river—that vital energy needed for starting life. I have been interested in body energy for many years, beginning through experiencing chronic fatigue. I am still amazed at the body's capability of connecting to flow, to energy and being energized, or having energy stifled and finding times of no energy. Hokhmah as the point of source, of making life happen, can be an encouragement, especially in this world where fatigue is a major issue, a knowing that when we go deeper, we find a source of life-energy (sometimes referred to as "subtle energy").

Hildegard of Bingen, in her mystical and imaginative way, captures in her writings Wisdom as this source, as life-giving breath that kindles the spark of life, fanning into flame:

> I am the supreme fiery force
> That kindles every spark of life;
> What I have breathed on will never die . . .
> I flame out—intense, godly Life—over the shining fields of corn
> I glow in the shimmer of the fire's embers,
> I burn in the sun and the moon and the stars.
> The secret Life of Me breathes in the wind
> And holds all things together soulfully.
> I am life in all its abundance,
> In me is the root of life.[8]

We can notice our energy often through the shifts in energy in our body; when we are aware of an increase in energy and when we notice a drain in energy. There will also be times when our energy flows well, often when we are doing something we love, linking to our particular gifts.

Energy is produced, through our neurotransmitters, from all our bodily interactions. All our thoughts and our emotions affect our energy:

> As our feelings change, this mixture of peptides travels through your body and your brain. And they are literally changing the chemistry of every cell in your body.[9]

Emotion is composed of energy that continually pours through us, setting in motion deep processes that affect every aspect of our life. Understanding more of our emotions helps us with this energy. We can develop emotional intelligence through self-awareness of both our mood and our thoughts about our mood.

The most primitive part of our brain, the limbic system, is the part that is involved in emotional responses. It was over many years that our brains enlarged and the thinking brain, or neocortex, developed. The limbic system worked well for our ancestors, ensuring the survival of the human race, developing as the rational brain emerged.

The root of the word "emotion" is *movere*, the Latin verb "to move", plus the prefix "e-" to connote "move away", suggesting that emotions are impulses to act. Children and animals show us these impulses, coming suddenly from the limbic brain. By adulthood, we have a varied reaction depending on our emotional intelligence and our past experience. Some guests at Holy Rood House have had traumatic experiences and trauma can keep triggering emotions and images, keeping the person in a traumatic state. Noticing helps us to step away from getting caught up in the emotional state and images, and to be aware of what is happening in the body—to the energy and state of the body. This noticing triggers a different part of the brain, the thinking brain, where we can learn to understand impulsive emotions. This is the rational mind meeting with the emotional mind, creating the wise mind mentioned in the previous chapter.

The energy from emotions is dependent on the emotion. Emotions just are: I don't like to refer to them as positive or negative emotions. However, some emotions generate more energy than others. Anger, for instance, creates strong energy; sadness decreases our energy; fear and anxiety can keep the body on alert and take us into the fight or flight response, which stifles opening to Wisdom's process. Emotions such as compassion, happiness, thankfulness and love can create the opposite of this response, can calm, lead to contentment and more energy:

> Bodies are often mistrusted because they are home to our feelings. Our emotions don't come in discrete packets: aliveness is a function of the whole "system" of my being. If I repress my anger, I stifle my joy: if I deny my grief, I withhold my capacity for empathy and delight.[10]

Emotions also cause a shift in energy that we can notice throughout the day. What has shifted our mood? As we come into the deep body-knowing we notice what reactions in the body the emotion brings, and perhaps the message of the emotion; for emotions are the messengers of the body.

As a Spiritual Director/Accompanier, I am alert to the Wisdom process of those I listen to in the one-to-one setting or in the groups I manage. How has that guest changed mood, made that decision, kept going through suffering? We also consider the season the body is currently going through; this might be a season connected to the body such as the menopause or a health issue, or one related to particular seasons in our life such as losses and spiritual health. Grief can be a season of many years, and our spiritual health will fluctuate through our life happenings. As we learn to pause throughout our day to notice changes in moods, thoughts and our creative happenings, we also consider the life we are living and the season we are travelling through.

Noticing—connecting us to a deeper centre of identity
The observer stance is the noticer; what we notice, within and around ourselves, links us to the present moment and what our bodies are receiving in that moment. Dr Roberto Assagioli, the founder of Psychosynthesis, studied this sense of observer with its connection to a deeper centre of identity named as the "I" or personal self.[11] This is our true essence behind all our masks and conditionings. The noticer connects us to this "I", this core centre from which there is coordination and connection of our diverse inner elements, giving us a sense of centredness and identity. This identity is our true identity, one that does not rely on our roles. Here is the core centre that is not worker, parent, child, lover, friend—perhaps a non-identity—where Wisdom brings forth our truth.

The "I" or personal self is researched in psychological practices and in various faiths. There is a story of Meister Eckhart getting in touch with his "I" centre. There was one day when he got really down and said to himself "I am frustrated with myself". It was this statement that made him realize he had found he had an "I" and a "self"; that led him to a very interesting journey. He asked himself: "Who is the narrator in my head at the moment? Is it the "I" that connects and belongs in the world, or is it the "Self" that gets in the way?"[12]

Our "I" has home in our spaciousness, our sacred core. Our "I" is revealed through Hokhmah, Holy Wisdom or the "sacred sense". Hokhmah/Sophia exists as the first Interior Experience before creation came about:

I—the first Interior Experience—
joined the journey from the very start.
This was the first and most ancient mystery:
how the power of growth can be contained
and fixed around a centre,
the identity of the self.
This is the axis on which the universe turns.[13]

Our "I" is that pivotal point within the turning universe, or as T. S. Eliot expresses it, a still point where there is neither movement from, nor towards, up or down, but only the dance:

Except for the point, the still point,
There would be no dance, and there is only the dance.[14]

For a retreat I was organizing which included this pivotal point, I wanted to find an image to illustrate this complex revealing. I found a superb video of time-lapse photography focused on the North Star in the night sky.[15] The North Star is seen as the pivotal point around which all the other stars revolve, perhaps illustrating the "I" of the first Interior Experience of Hokhmah. We are not usually aware of the movement of the earth, and this short clip highlights that unfelt movement. Another still point would be the camera that was set to take photos every few seconds, perhaps representing our own "I". As we notice a deeper sense of identity, Wisdom enables a perception of the dance that is within the wider connection in the cosmos.

Hokhmah/Sophia is the "I-ness" that is at the core of all beings, of every living being on our planet, uniting all beings and beingness into a greater unity. The noticing process initiates a way for us to connect our "I-ness" to the "I-ness" of others, of creation and of the Enabler of creation—the Life beyond all life.

In the book of Exodus, the story is told of Moses called to rescue the captured Israelites from the Egyptians. Moses was trying to fathom what to say to the Israelites when they asked who had sent him. Moses could not find the right expression for the name of "God", an issue with which many of us may resonate. The reply he heard was "I am who I am" and "Thus you shall say to the Israelites, 'I am' has sent me to you." The hearing continued with an added comment to say to the Israelites that *YHWH* has sent me to you. YHWH is the unnameable name which is not pronounced in Jewish prayers. The four letters lead to a variety of meanings including expressing ever-living Life, in the past, present and future. The roots express action, a sense of dance, rather than a state of being; it is simultaneity—the past, present and future are one—The-Being-who-is-who-was-and-who-will-be. In the Exodus verses YHWH is connected with the verb *hayah* which means "to be": "I will be what I will be."[16]

We have many guests come to Holy Rood House who have had instilled in them to look outward and upward for a connection to "God". God is often talked about as being "out there" and "in heaven". When we are exploring our own spirituality and the connection to greater unity, we may consider the mystery that encompasses all our believing. Connecting to process, to action, to the present moment, may be as-yet unexplored ways to understand our faith.

Encouraging our noticing of Wisdom in process

Expectation and spaces

Our noticing needs to link with a sense of expectation of an inner way of knowing that goes beyond our rational understanding and will bring about a way of transformation that encompasses our heart, mind, body and spirit. We are led into an awareness of a process that takes us beyond the everyday life, the surface babble of problems and chaos. It is exciting and brings energy and motivation.

The right spaces and pace are needed for this exploration. Although noticing can be quick—through a pause, a breath, a connection to our body—we also need slower times that we put aside throughout the day and the week, times to listen through our noticings and find a way to connect to our "I". Etty Hillesum describes a way of "soaking" that helped her in her suffering life for her transforming:

> ... that is probably the only right way with literature, with study,
> with people or with anything else: to let it all soak in, to let it all

mature slowly inside you until it has become a part of yourself. That, too, is a growing process. Everything is a growing process. And in between, emotions and sensations that strike you like lightning. But still the most important thing is the organic process of growing.[17]

Compassionate attention

Noticing will bring up aspects such as thoughts, emotions, energies, which may surprise, bring joy, may shock, or disappoint. Our noticing needs to link to a compassionate attention, a loving of ourselves as we listen and observe. We are aware that all emotions contain seeds of Wisdom; we notice with nurturing rather than getting involved in the emotion itself.

There are many practices that enable this compassionate attention, such as meditation, mindfulness and prayer. Whatever practice we try, it needs to be one that suits our personality, our energy and how we tick. Our noticing may lead to a letting go and surrendering of the armour we may have acquired over the years, our clinging on to ways that are not serving us. We may like to have practices with others. I meet with one of the chaplains at Holy Rood House for a weekly half hour to listen to Wisdom, as well as Sunday meeting at Quakers, where we listen and notice in the held quietness. Both feel a vital part of my week. At Holy Rood House, we encourage a way of noticing, especially through the creative process; we offer practices to support these noticings, such as evening prayers that end with a time of quiet with lit candles, meditation spaces, stilling practice, and other ways of prayerfulness.

Creativity and journaling

Connecting to a creative activity, especially one that allows flow, play and experimenting, can be helpful to encourage our noticing. We can try any creative activity that appeals and notice what is evoked. It involves taking the sense of play and exploration while we sit with some colour and materials in front of us, play an instrument, or go out into a garden with our senses alive. As we touch, smell, colour, stitch, mould, pluck, we listen to what is going on for us in the process. There may be frustrations as to what is emerging, emotions that are stirred, memories that come to the fore. Although the outcome is not the important part of this process, there will be an end to the exploration, and pausing to reflect on what has happened in the creating can aid insight into our present lives. As with all practices, more insights will come as we get used to exploring and reflecting.

Having a notebook, maybe with plain paper, where writing and colour can be used, is a very helpful way to develop our noticings. Jotting down what we are attracted to, exploring what has stirred our emotions, what helps our energy, and noting our journey of opening to Wisdom, perhaps through the creative ideas in this book, can help us consolidate and highlight the way of Wisdom. As we mark our noticings, we learn more about who we are, our uniqueness, gifts, what turns us on, and what gets us through difficulties. It is easy to forget the glimpses of encouragement, love and learning in our life journey; marking these in some way adds depth in our lives, helping us move below the surface of the everyday.

Our journals can be a place of experimenting. One of my journal entries marked my exploring of conversing with my intuition, listening whilst using a rhythmical practice of weaving. From this quiet place, I felt my intuition would say:

I am allowed, I am. I come into being.
I come through a flow, through a depth, a grounding.
I am a hopeful place.
Find the I am, I am in the I am; in the moment, in the stillness, in what I notice in nature.

One of our community who is a musician often improvises on the keyboard, describing this as being taken on a journey that involves his emotions, never being quite sure where the music leads, and knowing he will not be in the same frame of mind and spirit as when he started. It can be elating as well as exhausting. When guests are listening to his improvising, he finds that others respond to the pieces he chooses as they pick up a flavour of the creative process. We can notice what resonates with us as we connect to others' creativity, through music, art, poetry and what catches our eye and ear.

Our community often has exhibitions in our gallery space. One embroidery exhibition—Meaningful embroideries—had over 30 hand- and machine-embroidered pieces exploring the environment, justice and peace. I encouraged one visiting group to notice which picture or pictures resonated with them; to go with the body senses and feel what colours, textures, titles stirred a reaction. One woman stated that she usually glanced at exhibitions, and would have been in and out in three minutes. This unfamiliar process had really made the creations more personal to her, and she went away excited and resolved to look in detail and more personally at other art. Studies have found that visitors to art galleries spend an average of eight seconds looking at each work on display. Slow looking had encouraged more resonance, a personal opening for this guest.

Another woman had contrasting feedback from this display. She had been struck by a few lines of a poem introduced before the exhibition:

> We look too closely, seeing only strands and knots and
> snarled threads of too-much-trying or none-at-all.
> Grant us eyes to see the whole of which we are a part.[18]

This resonated with her intruding niggles at the issues that were not right for her, especially in her church. She appreciated standing back and looking at the embroideries as a whole.

As we explore creatively, we can uncover symbols and images that bring their own energy through their enlightening.[19] As we stand back to look at our noticings, we may see a pattern, leading to an integrity, like pieces of a jigsaw coming together. In the writing of this book, so many small elements have joined to make a bigger picture, expressing far more than I had imagined.

There are many interesting cultural and biblical symbols of Wisdom that can inspire creative exploration. Our dreams can give a huge creative resource to explore and open to Wisdom and there is a section in Appendix 3 to encourage exploration with our dreams.

Exploring our "I am"

As we become more aware of our inner "I", we can develop the connection this gives us to a sense of fulfilment and purpose within ourselves, and a way of listening to our needs. In my journalings, I try and explore my noticings that connect me to my true identity:

> I feel most connected to my "I" in my early morning risings—this
> sense of connection with the core of myself, as I sink into my
> body. Something happens in these special times and the "I" seems
> to lead in my writing, walking in the dark, doing some yoga,
> with the body opening to minister to my needs. These times
> may be short, yet still enable a meeting deep within. Keeping
> a connection to the core "I" connects me to the earth and
> belonging. The "I" integrates what the day brings to me—the
> offerings of what comes up; often very different to what I forecast.

There are many metaphors and symbols of the "I am" centre within us
that help us to explore this sacred spaciousness. Jesus, with his direct
connection to Hokhmah/Sophia Wisdom, illuminates these "I am"
statements highlighted in many sacred writings, including the Gospel
of John. Jesus, in the Aramaic language, uses the expression "I of I" to
express the uniting of Holy Wisdom, our "I", with the "I" of the Holy
One, connecting us to cosmic unity.[20] The different aspects of the "I
am" that Jesus taught (for example the eight "I am" statements in John's
Gospel[21]) connect to different elements and aspects of our sensory selves
illuminating our body-knowing and connecting our own sense of "I"
with Life and the Everlasting life-energy. They can be read with our own
"I am" connection.

For example, in John 10:9 Jesus voices the aspect of the "I am" as
the door—an aspect within our embodied selves where there is free
movement. Through this door, we find the Source, the connection with
life-energy that Jesus is teaching, which gives us space or "pasture" to
find rest and relief. The "I am" as bread gives us the feeding we need
of renewable life-energy; the "I am" as shepherd illustrates the guiding
and nurturing of the "I am". Other "I am" statements encourage the
transformation process, the new birth that emerges through Holy
Wisdom.

We can explore writings that try and articulate the great mystery of
faith and encourage Wisdom (suggestions in Appendix 2). The Austrian
poet Rainer Maria Rilke tried to express the unsayable and the invisible
with an intimate connection of God as the "deep innerness of all things".[22]

He described God as the one who is coming, a fulfilment, unfolding through us as the future unfolds:

> What stops you from living your life as a painful and beautiful day in the history of an immense pregnancy? Do you not see how all that is happening is ever again a new beginning?[23]

Subtle energy work

We become aware of the movement of subtle energies, through our ways of attention, through creative process and through listening within our deeper spaciousness. All of creation has an energy, where Wisdom flows, often referred to as vibrations, that we can be made more aware of through a way of Wisdom.

There is a vast range of energy practices and therapies now offered that can help free up our deeper energies, bringing healing and more awareness of our energy, such as yoga, massage, acupressure, tai chi, qigong, sound healing and many others. It is trying what we are drawn to and what sits well with our beliefs. The Capacitar organization has many simple tools to encourage and explore our energy and Wisdom.[24]

To conclude this section, I would like to encourage those who may be finding some of the ideas in this chapter tricky or somewhat alien. Many of the aspects written about in this chapter (some of which have given me hours of deliberating!) will be fleshed out during the following chapters. Wisdom is worth pursuing; in connecting to process, to energy, to deep innerness, we find that Wisdom's revealing can yield abundant fruit:

Wisdom praises herself:

> "Like the vine I bud forth delights,
> and my blossoms become glorious and abundant fruit.
> Come to me, you who desire me,
> and eat your fill of my fruits.
> For the memory of me is sweeter than honey
> and the possession of me sweeter than the honeycomb.
> Those who eat of me will hunger for more,
> and those who drink of me will thirst for more."[25]

Creative ideas for this chapter

Connecting to our spaciousness with compassionate attention
We take time to get comfortable, to switch off from phones and other distractions.

We have a sense of expectation, as we put aside this time to breathe, connect to our deep body-knowing and open to a deeper space.

We use our breath to breathe in slower and deeper. We feel the grounding of the chair and floor. We may like to get nearer the floor and lie outstretched.

We imagine an opening as we breathe, an opening into a spaciousness within. As we breathe in, the way opens, and as we breathe out, we breathe out any clutter.

We breathe in and open, we breathe out and clear.

We bring a compassionate presence into this space. We listen through the ears of nurture, and notice through the eyes of love.

We imagine dropping into this spaciousness where Wisdom moves.

We listen, we notice, within this spaciousness.

This is a spaciousness that connects to our "I am", our true essence. We meet our truth, ourselves with no baggage, no stress and no complications, and relax within this truth.

We imagine an energy radiating from this centre, an energy connecting to our life-force. We bask in this energy, perhaps imagining it as the energy from the sun shining within, or a colour that is right for us.

We let ourselves be held within this energy.

We connect to the oneness of this space, a oneness experienced throughout creation. Here Wisdom holds us in connection with all creation, held in unity and love.

If possible, we stay for a few minutes with this compassionate attention.

We may like to add a hum, finding a note that resonates from this spaciousness, our unique note.

Take time to come to and perhaps note anything that has come up for you.

When I did a similar exercise in a group, one guest found when her hum was in a lower register it felt more resonant. As she hummed and got distracted by thoughts her hum got higher and didn't sound good, perhaps more strained. She also said that her cat looked at her very strangely as she did this hum; she had never seen this expression on her cat's face before!

"I am" Prayer

I am tearful;
may my tearfulness be prayerful.

I am prayerful;
may my prayerfulness be hopeful.

I am hopeful;
may my hopefulness be joyful.

I am joyful;
may my joyfulness be playful.

I am playful;
may my playfulness be mindful.

I am mindful;
may my mindfulness be restful.

I am restful;
may my restfulness be peaceful.

I am peaceful;
I am peace.[26]

Notes

1   Doris Klein, *Journey of the Soul* (Lanham, MD: Sheed & Ward, 2000), p. 47.

2   *Hildegard of Bingen's Scivias: Know the Ways*, tr. Bruce Hozeski (Sante Fe, CA: Bear & Company, 1986), p. xx.

3   Neil Douglas-Klotz, *Desert Wisdom: A Nomad's Guide to Life's Big Questions from the Heart of the Native Middle East* (Worthington: ARC Books, 2011), p. 301.

4   Matthew Fox, *Meister Eckhart: A Mystic Warrior for our Times* (Novato, CA: New World Library, 2014), p. 122.

5   Author, 2020, previously unpublished.

6   Cynthia Bourgeault, *The Wisdom Way of Knowing: Reclaiming an Ancient Tradition to Awaken the Heart* (Hoboken, NJ: Jossey-Bass, 2003), pp. 48–9.

7   Wisdom 7:24.

8   Hildegard of Bingen from one of her hymns, as cited in Seyyed Hossein Nasr, *Religion and the Order of Nature* (New York, NY: Oxford University Press, 1996), p. 59.

9   Dr Candace Pert, <https://www.6seconds.org/2007/01/26/the-physics-of-emotion-candace-pert-on-feeling-good/>.

10   Alex Wildwood, *A Faith to Call my Own* (London: Quaker Home Service, 1999), p. 34.

11   Piero Ferrucci, *What We May Be: Techniques for Psychological and Spiritual Growth through Psychosynthesis* (New York: Tarcher/Penguin, 2004), p. 64.

12   Story from an On Being podcast, <https://onbeing.org/series/podcast/>.

13   From an interpretive translation of Proverbs 8:22 by Douglas-Klotz, *Desert Wisdom*, p. 113.

14   T. S. Eliot, *Four Quartets* (London: Faber & Faber, 1944), p. 5.

15   North Star (Star Trails) © "Jamie" 2014, <https://www.youtube.com/watch?v=tp6UkqIwVfk>.

16   Exodus 3:14; Douglas-Klotz, *Desert Wisdom*, p. 284.

17   Etty Hillesum, *An Interrupted Life: The Diaries, 1941–1943*, tr. Het Verstoorde Leven (New York: Pantheon Books, 1983), p. 86.

18   Pat Kozak and Janet Schaffran, <https://danceforallpeople.com/weaver-god-weave-my-life-into-yours/>.

[19] For more about journaling and creative ideas see my book *Finding your Inner Treasure: A Spiritual Journey of Creative Exploration* (New Town Farm: Kevin Mayhew, 2010).

[20] Notes on an interpretation of John 8:12, see Douglas-Klotz, *Desert Wisdom*, p. 270.

[21] The "I am" statements of Jesus can be found in John's Gospel—6:35; 8:12 and 58; 10:9 and 11; 11:25; 14:6 and 15:1.

[22] <https://www.goodreads.com/quotes/843754-you-are-the-deep-innerness-of-all-things-the-last>.

[23] Rome, December 23, 1903, *Letters to a Young Poet*, trs and eds Anita Barrows and Joanna Macy, *A Year with Rilke: Daily Readings from the Best of Rainer Maria Rilke* (New York: HarperCollins, 2009), January 31st entry.

[24] <https://capacitar.org/>.

[25] Sirach (or Ecclesiasticus) 24:1,17–21.

[26] Elizabeth Baxter, *I am noticing* prayer, *Holy Rood House Community Prayer* (independently published, 2017), p. 24.

CHAPTER 3

Wisdom calls through community

We reach for a welcome

We reach for a welcome that beckons us homeward,
crossing the threshold to find safer space,
a place we can turn to in hurt and rejection,
where tender compassion bears witness to grace.

We rest in a love that can offer us healing,
care for the aching and comfort for pain,
a gentle embrace of our wounds and our rawness,
protecting our frailty through suffering and strain.

We long for a wisdom that answers our searching,
the questions that baffle and agonized cries,
the mystery behind all our anger and stumbling
in darkness that hides all the path from our eyes.

We sing of a hope that is flourishing in us,
shaping our lives into all they might be,
delighting in art and in music and laughter,
the God of creation in joy sets us free.[1]

As we open to our spaciousness we link to the flow of Wisdom like a spring
or river. In this chapter, we explore Wisdom as this flow, connecting to
all—creatures, earth and cosmos. We explore how we support each other
in our flow and in our stagnant times through community, and how
community can encourage the voice of this flow.

This opening hymn is one we sing at Holy Rood House, and the elements of this song will be highlighted through the chapter, alongside how we, as a community, learn the Wisdom way, alongside our guests. We open the exploration of Wisdom in community by noting that we all have a community within ourselves. Our personality is not a unified oneness; it is made up of different aspects that we can bring to the fore to receive the Wisdom of these aspects. Roberto Assagioli, in the psychological principles of Psychosynthesis, suggests that we have a whole village within us, and these aspects of our personality, or psychological satellites, he named as subpersonalities. We modify our thoughts to different situations. Sometimes life feels doable, sometimes scary; our outlook changes regularly, often with our mood. When we look to our subpersonalities we are connecting to our prominent traits, moods, attitudes or motives; how we tackle various situations in our lives.

Noting that we have different aspects of ourselves can be helpful in exploring our reactions—to events and with other relationships:

> We are not unified; we often feel that we *are*, because we do not have many bodies and many limbs, and because one hand doesn't usually hit the other. But, metaphorically, that is exactly what does happen within us. Several subpersonalities are continually scuffling: impulses, desires, principles, aspirations are engaged in an unceasing struggle.[2]

I accompanied a guest who mentioned that she often felt like Jekyll and Hyde. There were two parts of her that felt like they were pulling her in different directions. In this session, I brought out a basket of characters that I have collected through various charity shops—plastic animals, soft toys, dolls, for example—and she picked out two pieces that seemed to represent these two aspects of herself. These important aspects of herself could be explored through the characters themselves, understanding more of what they represented and most importantly what they needed.

Fleshing out a subpersonality as a character can be a helpful way of understanding this part of our "village", and there is a creative exercise at the end to enable this exploration. We can go through our lives with one aspect of ourselves running our lives. This is important to note. We may be functioning with an anxious part of us dictating the way we make decisions and manage our life, for example. We may feel that this part is who we are. As we collate different aspects of ourselves, we can notice other parts of us that add to our identity and that can help balance and integrate our lives. They can put into context the parts of us that seem to take over. We can have conversations between the different aspects of us, so that each part can start to understand the other. There will be reasons for each of our subpersonalities, and each will have its helpful and not so helpful ways. This is done with kindness, as all parts of ourselves need to feel loved.

For myself, exploring subpersonalities has been eye-opening. One of the earlier characters that emerged through my move into community was that of a grey mare—an intuitive presence that I often imagined to notice her reactions, what startles her and how she ministers to me. She was, and is, a great encouragement with her gentle strength and presence. I name all the characters I explore, and this naming seems to come from an intuitive place. Freya came to mind for my grey mare, and I was moved when I found the meaning of her name to be Goddess of Love and Poetry. Likewise, I have explored the secretary part of myself—the organizer who can get a bit bossy and gets my brain chuntering over plans and issues. I named her Avaleen, a name that came to me without thought and with a sense of her "leanness". Unsure that it was a name, I was surprised to find it is Greek for Goddess of Wisdom and War (a derivative of Athena). My secretary self is good at dominating, and I have to tell her to quiet at times, so my thoughts can relax and I can switch off from work mode. When angry, I have explored that mood as a character, my nature boy is a part of me that enjoys the wild, and my dancer is one that is exuberant and loves to stretch. These can link with Jung's archetypes of the child, wise person, artist, leader, nurturer, jester, lover, magician and explorer, for instance.

By bringing the characters that we have explored together we will have a circle of inner Wisdom. Collating parts of ourselves we can notice how they help and inform us, and bring them into this sense of Hokhmah, of Holy Wisdom, the integrator, one who holds all parts of ourselves in love.

Our subpersonalities all come together through the observer, the noticer that connects to our "I", as introduced in the last chapter.

Hokhmah/Sophia is the "I-ness" at the core of all beings, bringing our own subpersonalities into a unity within us and a wider unity around us, calming that *unceasing struggle* and helping us feel more integrated. We are not individual; we have a belonging to the earth and a connection to all creatures.

Hokhmah's life-spark is there at our conception. We are beings in relation right from the start through the joining of the egg and sperm. The word *consciousness* has a root meaning of "knowing-with", and all that we become aware of is in relation with our "I-ness". Opening out to Wisdom can help us to have this relationship with our bodies, which can be one of our foremost difficult relationships. Many of us have disconnected from our sense of self through a lifetime of giving to others, without the time or way of connecting to this primary relationship. The process of knowing comes from the process of relating. How do we relate to our own body—when it is healthy and not so healthy?

It is important to remember that Wisdom is a felt sense and when we connect in relationship it is through our sensing. It is often the quality of aliveness, found in all living beings, that draws us into relationship. Whether we are holding a baby, exploring in nature, communing with animals, we can open to relationship, and explore the nature of Wisdom through relationship.

As the Community of Holy Rood House, we work with the delicate task of accompanying people who are re-connecting with their own personhood. We know that each guest already has a relationship with the deep knowing within, and we try and encourage this relationship. It is through the importance of hospitality, of valuing each guest, that we connect our own "I-ness" to the "I am" of those we meet. Each day, our community changes, as new guests arrive and we have a different combination of staff, and together we open to receive the Wisdom of that moment. The community is kept alive through this movement of Wisdom—bringing hope and renewal each day.

It is our early relationship with our mother and family, expanding to friends, teachers, our pets, environment and our communities that are key components of our identity. When we welcome guests at Holy Rood House, we use their name; we acknowledge who they are. We welcome from our own Wisdom centre, with this connection to love. We are not welcoming another in their roles—whatever work they do, or as carer, mother, or health state. We are welcoming the guest as they are in the now, acknowledging that both ourselves as the welcomer and the welcomed are together in community. There is something in this connection of relationship that is empowering to both.

Diverse relationships can enhance different aspects of ourselves. One story to illustrate this is of a three-year-old boy who was part of the community, and his engagement with one of the guests at Holy Rood House. The child was used to the variety of guests visiting the house. One visitor, an older woman, came in deep depression. She was getting help from the counselling team and the community, and yet often sat immobile in a chair in the lounge, unable to motivate or engage with what went on around her. One day this child went up to her, patted her on the arm and said slowly "It's alright, it's alright". Something in that connection, in that relationship, stirred the woman, created that spark that was needed for her to change. From that moment she started the journey to connect to herself and her needs, to move outwards and do what she needed to do. The boy, connected to his Senser, his Wisdom, reached out and in that reaching out with touch and tender words, relationship happened and the guest was able to open to Wisdom's flow.

Something new emerges out of the encounters that we have with each other. Because we are beings in relation, we are always coming into being; in this movement of becoming. Change is inevitable, hopefully for the better. The guests find that often their interaction with another guest can have a transformative effect. In the creative environment that we encourage many conversations can lift and excite, engaging Wisdom's energy. One week we had a young guest that helped to encourage a new guest as they found, in a jewellery making session, that they had creativity in common. The jewellery making brought them together with a shared interest and helped them to form a friendship that developed throughout the week. We had another guest arrive later in the week. She came to the creative writing session on the Thursday where we were exploring the wise voice within. She had been sharing with the younger guest about her love of nature. They both discovered that they liked the plants, trees and wildlife and this young guest offered to show her some of the crocuses in the garden. They both had a special time in the garden, whilst the younger guest showed her flowers and plants, textures and colours that they both appreciated. As the older guest recounted this connection, during the writing exercise, she named the voice of this young guest as her wise voice.

Rowan Williams in his book *Being Human* encourages us to seek to set up relationship, as there is no part of ourselves that is not in relationship. He recognizes the courage this takes and assures *that we are related already to something that holds us, engages us and carries us through (with ourselves and others).*[3] Wisdom holds us in connection with all creation, held in unity and love. Community is built on relationship; we try and speak from this held connection, recognizing that each person in community can connect to Wisdom holder, with the connection to love in the other.

Julian of Norwich, the fourteenth-century anchoress who wrote *Revelations of Divine Love,* saw the three persons of the Trinity as Strength, Wisdom and Love. This dynamic trio is the enabling of relationship and the holding within us that keeps us going. Julian goes on to state that her soul was taught most about love. Love is more than an emotion and a value; whereas Wisdom has been referred to the underground spring or river, love is the bedrock, the firm foundation, that undergirds the spaciousness of the wise mind. Love is a connector through ourselves, to others and the environment. Gandhi was a testament to the enduring power of love. He said that love should permeate every aspect of our lives and that all human activities should be informed by love.[4] Saint Paul wrote:

> [Love] bears all things, believes all things, hopes all things, endures all things.[5]

I am a Quaker and find in our Sunday worship, sitting in the silence for an hour, with others, there is a holding connecting me to love. As we open our inner ears and eyes, opening to an inner depth, we wait in "love and truth".[6] We are able to sit with the immensities of what is going on in our own lives, in the lives of our loved ones and in the chaos of the world by sitting with these realities, knowing that we are held in love. This is love that we can receive from each other, from the people we think of and the presence of love connecting within the silence of the meeting. At root it is a love that holds us in the world:

> Prayer is not words or acts, but reaching down to love: holding our fellows in love, offering ourselves in love; and being held by, being caught up in love. It is communion, an opening of the door, an entry from the beyond. This is the point where secular language fails, for this cannot be spoken about at all: it can only be known.[7]

From this depth of love that grounds our being and holds us in relationship, Wisdom is able to flow. If we keep to ourselves and do not connect to earth, creature or human, our flowing spring may become stagnant. I learnt during the long chronic illness I had that I needed to keep my connection to those who were wanting to share their love, however hard that was for me at times, otherwise I became very introverted and morbid. I had to learn to leap the hurdle of asking, sharing and receiving, realizing that I could not heal on my own. This is also important to us as a community at Holy Rood House. When one member is feeling low, unable to give out too much, then we try and come together to help hold the hope and encourage.

Julian also states that compassion keeps us in this love. The words "community" and "compassion" come from the same root, denoting "together, beside". Compassion, literally meaning "suffering with another" (and, according to Meister Eckhart, the best of all the names we have for "God"), comes from the ground of love. Wisdom opens us to being tender-hearted, to feeling the sorrow of others:

> Compassion is a kind and gentle property that belongs to the Motherhood in tender love. Compassion protects, increases our sensitivity, gives life, and heals.[8]

We find the movement of relation and compassion connects our community of diverse people. Out of this empathic movement comes a sense of justice, especially as many of our guests are marginalized and in circumstances that are unjust. Justice requires Wisdom from our intuition, as well as knowledge from our rational nature. It requires both the maternal compassion and the energy of the radical.

Through being open to Wisdom in ways of relationship, listening, prayer, creativity, wellbeing and learning we become a prophetic voice for those on the margins and a place of healing of ourselves and the earth. It is as we come together with our guests that this prophetic voice arises and gives to others what already belongs to them; the seeds lying dormant within are watered and there is an awakening to what we are and can become.

Wisdom becomes a fire that connects and stokes our passions as we awaken to the injustices around us. I can really relate to this energy coming from a community with a mission (and also supported by the Quaker community that is very active with social justice). I have a constant urge to do and say what needs to be activated, and the writing of this book has come out of this dynamic energy:

> The fire in the head is an inner fire . . . It's a fire that wakes you up at night and penetrates your darkest spaces, burns off the psychological crap, freeing energy and inspiration to attempt the otherwise unthinkable.
>
> The nuns of St Bridgit nursed this sacred fire. It is what gives life radiance, what makes the sun and other stars go round . . . It is the origin of poesis (the making)—the silver nectar of the Tree of Life—the very passion of creation.[9]

As a community working on the margins, stories are an important aspect of sharing Wisdom and we try and listen with the ear of love, rather than impatience or unbelief. This is often in the privacy of a meeting with a pastoral listener, or in an organized group retreat. Although we all have our own prejudices and judgements, we try to be open to other perspectives and to go with what is voiced, especially knowing how all stories add to the Wisdom of community. The stories of minorities, ones not often heard, and the raw pain stories can be the most difficult and maybe the most important to be heard.

When I was going through my chronic illness, I needed to go to a place where I could hear the suffering story—one of lament, with no happy ending, perhaps of someone that was going through the pain with which I could resonate. My church at that time was not this place—I heard no honest stories about the difficulties arising in others and the world. When we hear hardship stories at Holy Rood House, we are witnesses to that story—we hear it and it is affirmed. We do not offer platitudes or "a God" who will sort out issues; we trust the witnessing process—what we would term "with-ness"—how through hearing the story, and sitting with "what is", we are held together in a greater Wisdom that comes out of the "is-ness", the hearing with each other.

On one retreat day, a woman in the art room started a doodle with paint and brush. She couldn't find the black paint so used purple. She then found the black paint and added to the doodle. She saw some upsetting things in the doodle and had a chat with me, getting reassurance that she did not have to show her painting to others. From this sharing, she then saw other spaces to add other colours. Later on, having developed the painting, another guest remarked how beautiful it was. The painter guest was affected by this very different perspective.

We had some feedback time later in the day, and there were two comments that helped to add to the perspective of her picture. One comment was a story about a man giving a lecture who drew a black dot on a big sheet of white paper and asked what the students could see. Most said a black dot, rather than the vast whiteness of the paper. Another comment was someone talking about colour.

When it came to the Chapel space in the evening, there was a chance for guests to bring their creations into this prayerful space. The painter guest decided to take her painting into the Chapel, where it would be seen. She was able to voice the process of what had happened in the art room and how the comments of the guests had helped her perspective (especially the guest saying it was beautiful). She realized that there was more to her picture than just the distressing images that she could see, another perspective was coming through the pure white and the boundary of the paper, which for her was a sense of divinity.

Many of our guests live isolated lives, and yet as they come into community they find they become the midwives/persons for each other, which encourages all in our community. We come together in a mutual way of working; the staff are hosts and also can be guests as we are the listeners and receive from guests. Often what the guests say adds to our vision, and adds to the movement of the community for that week.

The stories that guests bring continue the hope and healing of the whole community. For some, it is the stories of others that keep them connected in difficult times and help them feel less isolated in their pain. This poem, created on a group retreat, sums up some of the experience of storytelling in community:

> Sowing seeds of justice, memory making stories
> kept alive, struggling to be told amidst a
> rushing, noisy, disinterested society of self first.
> Stories to open the chasm, lifting out of the depths
> a grace-filled conscious-raising people, set free.
>
> Sowing seeds of justice, with love encompassing all
> in peace, acceptance, deepening the "I am", me.
> Sending out ripples of light, growth, seeds to burst forth,
> littering the earth with colour, diversity, hope, peace.[10]

In my listening and reflecting with guests, together we open to the dynamic movement of Wisdom, the flow of Strength, Wisdom and Love, the dance of the Trinity, felt through the silent spaces, the energy changes, and enlightened ideas. This has increased my trust in my working as we leave the spaces that Wisdom needs for her emerging. I am constantly surprised by the healing energy in the spark of transformation that occurs—often in small ways, finding that I am frequently at my healthiest when working with guests; this is not what I would have envisaged when I moved into community:

> We all come from a place of pain and a place of peace and the sharing is a resurrection.[11]

Community is not always an easy place to be, especially with coping with vulnerability as we open to Wisdom's ways. When we are in this more vulnerable position, to open to the Wisdom of others means assessing any barriers that we put up to protect ourselves. We all need a certain degree of self-protection, and in community this needs to be flexible enough to allow in the Wisdom of others. If we hide behind a "brick wall" type of protection, which may be due to our past and what others may have done to us, we may not be open to the help of others. I suggest to many guests that they explore an image that is helpful for a more flexible way of relationship with others. Some explore an image of an invisible cloak—a sense of overall protection of the body. Others discover a swing gate image—one where a sense of closure can be obtained when we need to revitalize ourselves, with an opening when we are ready to receive from others. We also remember that our sacred spaciousness is always held and protected with the foundation of a love that is beyond our physical relationships.

Wisdom can be stifled by our own thoughts of how we have handled situations in relationship. As a community, we try not to give power or energy to mulling over what we should have done or said. When we feel we have said something inappropriate, maybe reacted out of anger or not done something when we felt we should, then we try and let go of unhelpful thoughts. We can regret many things, and yet mulling over and over what should or should not have been done does not help the situation. There is an honesty in knowing that we are human and have our failings. It is also a way to treat each other gently in the community— it is alright to not always do right, so we model a way of being "good enough". We have to trust that what was done in that moment was in that moment, and not let it affect the present-day moment. Wisdom emerges from our living, from our trials and errors and seeing how others deal with mishaps. We can never tell what repercussions our actions will produce in the movement of community that none can control. We can fail at something and let each other down, but in community there is a greater movement that envelops us—the Wisdom way, that needs us to step back and notice what happens.

We also realize that it is often those people who upset, anger or frustrate us most, who are our teachers. They are the ones reflecting a part of ourselves, a part that is upset, angry or frustrated. If we examine what irritates in others as something within ourselves, then we can become wiser about ourselves, and let community bring out different aspects of ourselves. By being a noticer of what stirs us with relationships, we can bring those noticings into our reflection space, perhaps exploring another of our subpersonalities, drawing out the Wisdom from these encounters. Community is more than our relationships with other humans. Our community at Holy Rood House includes our relationships with our pets (currently goats, dogs, hens and a tortoise) as well as the wildlife, garden and the surrounding environment. We are situated in two acres of land, close to the town centre of Thirsk, and near fields and a river. The buildings, consisting of two main houses, are part of the story and holding of Wisdom of the community. The richness of what has gone on in the houses and gardens is an important part of the expressions of what comes through in the present in community. We are mindful of the way the house and gardens are used, giving space and rest times for them to "breathe". The walls of the buildings are inanimate objects, and yet they hold something of the stories and prayers of the community, influencing the responses to what people hear.

When the coronavirus (Covid-19) pandemic started in 2020 and our community went into lockdown, we were unable to have guests to stay. The few of us who were residential kept vigilant to what was going on in ourselves, our community and the world. Stories of what was going on within our community were important to hear. The pandemic had thrown the world into huge transition, a liminal space: a not-yet, not-knowing stage—between the "how it was" and the "how it is going to be". There was a sense of needing to experience this transitional time, not to try and just get through it, but to experience and explore this "it". We tried to discover what this liminal space was offering, through our listening, learning and discussion. We worked out ways of supporting our staff and guests, so we could have the sense of travelling together through this time, to find a knowing-together.

This knowing-together is a way that Jesus highlighted to reassure his disciples when he knew of his death. "*I am* the Way" (John 14:6) reflects a way that links to the "I am" in each of us: the way that we can connect to the deep knowing of others. It is a relational way of knowing, connected to love and a reassurance that we are not alone. Support through phone calls, cards and emails became mutual as guests also sent their love and support; they were empowered to support us through the pandemic. We shared some of our Wisdom on our Facebook page, bringing in quotes, poems and the natural world. Support was also given through our chaplaincy and counselling service which was able to continue throughout all the lockdowns, in various forms.

We are also a community that expands virtually beyond our structures. Many of our guests find it a helpful concept to connect to the community from their own homes, in ways that help them feel supported. During the lockdowns of the Covid pandemic, the image of us all being strands in a big weaving—a weaving that encompasses community and goes out into the world—was a symbolic image. The image includes the truth that each thread is important and the sense that a piece is woven of our unique strands coming together. The discernment during this time gave us firm strands of Wisdom threads, alongside the strands of hope coming through many stories heard and our explorations. The fragile threads being held by the stronger threads and the sense of this weaving being integrated through love:

> Can creativity come out of chaos?
> Can chaos be beautiful?
> The answers, I think, to both are yes, but the chaos is so interwoven with pain that it is hard to find beauty or creativity.
> But a ray of light—I have in community with others woven a canopy which despite me is beautiful and perhaps my pain is woven in.[12]

Ideas for forming and exploring community

The way we connect to others and our environment will be very personal as our relationships depend on our past, our circumstances, our introversion and extroversion. The following are a few ideas for this exploration encouraging community.

Exploring our personal community and our environment
We may like to explore our inner community of subpersonalities, especially when we are aware of our mood, an attitude or a stirring from another relationship (see later exercise). These subpersonalities will help us consider the different aspects of ourselves. As we explore our

nurturing aspect we can let this balance our critical voice, giving us a wider perspective.

We may also consider our relationship with Wisdom, finding our own images and words to describe this movement. In experiencing relationship beyond the physical, we consider our spiritual experiences: our felt sense at a sunrise, our urge to think of others or listen, and the synchronicity that we experience. When we look out for events that appear significantly related, we revive the ancient Wisdom knowing of everything being connected. I shared a poem at one Quaker meeting, that was then brought to my poetry group three days later, although the bearer did not attend the Quaker meeting. Out of the hundreds of poems she could choose, she picked the one that had inspired me to speak in the silence, and one where we unearthed more Wisdom as we shared.

We may consider our connections with others, especially our supportive relationships, and expand this reflection to other creatures, to pets, wildlife, natural elements and our environment (explored further in Chapter 5).

Learning from discussion and differences

We can recognize that our own perspective and knowledge is limited by our upbringing, culture and learnings, so finding culturally diverse connections and differing ages, views and backgrounds will expand and enrich our thoughts and life. A smile, a kindness, a gentle question, being interested in another, can be the start of this relational movement.

In discussion, hearing ideas and beliefs other than our own can be viewed with an inquisitive mind. We may find open questions that aid conversation about others' interests and hopes. Relational Wisdom does not divide the world into religious and secular, but finds intrigue and mystery within the everyday. Theology that embraces Wisdom is one that is healing, transformative, celebratory, where we feel we can fly from restrictions or areas that shame us.

There are many books and ancient manuscripts that can highlight the different aspects of Wisdom to help our discussion. There are some suggestions in the bibliography. The Bible can be read seeking out the hidden presence of Wisdom—often in the spaces between the words or as splashes of colour that bring life—perhaps just taking a phrase to let it sink into our spaciousness. The theologian and author Margaret Barker has written and researched Holy Wisdom, developing an approach to biblical studies known as Temple Theology. As a "textual archaeologist", she has found Wisdom hidden throughout the Bible. The Hebrew texts, for example, were originally written without vowels, so the readers supplied the vowels and meaning. Not long after the start of Christianity the Hebrew text was fixed, to stop people changing the meaning, especially related to Holy Wisdom, or The Lady of the Temple, seen as idolatrous. In this way, religion could be more controlled with people excluded from the spiritual insight and understanding that comes from Holy Wisdom.[13]

There are many stories in these ancient manuscripts of minority people, hidden women, and abuse whose voices challenge justice for today and bring out the healing and hope of Wisdom. We can connect with some of the people in the Bible that highlight Wisdom, including Mary, the mother of Jesus, who reflects the Motherhood of Wisdom with nurturing gifts and a pondering heart.

We can find Wisdom people that help our own lives in our different seasons, in books, through creative arts, and the stories that we hear.

Opening to our unique voice

We have a unique contribution to knowledge through our experiences and our opening to Wisdom. Each of us is an important voice, a unique note in the chorus of the world. There is no-one else that would offer what we would say, as there is no other that has lived the life we have lived. There will be parts of our story, maybe of what we have noticed that has informed us, of transformative times, of encouragement, that will help another.

On a reflective garden day, we considered how we can flourish in dry times, bringing in the concept of this spring or flow within and connecting stories. As part of the day our resident gardener gave a demonstration of planting out succulents, plants that cope with dryness. With his calm voice, deliberate hands and clear instructions he had a captive audience, and everyone engaged with making their own planter. Later, in the feedback on the day, one guest shared her noticings, relating to the story we had shared of Moses striking the rock for the parched Israelites and letting water flow. She had noticed the same reaction in the story with the demonstration of the planting. For her, there was a similar process of the guests gathered around the succulent plants and the potting area, for the people gathered around that rock. The guests moving forward to make their pots, she realized, were somehow drinking from that life-giving water and something exciting was happening as people connected to soil and plants. As this guest spoke her noticings, there was a murmur of agreement from around the room. Her observations connected our group in that moment. It took her speaking out, articulating our felt sense, for all of us in the group to understand that we had been part of something exciting, something life-giving.

As we say what we see, perhaps of the bigger picture, we become the prophetic voice. This guest spoke out her noticings that helped others to recognize the process of Wisdom and the life this brings. This is how we come into new community, with our voicings of life-giving processes.

As we open to Wisdom, we can awaken to the many injustices in our times and can easily become overwhelmed. In finding the right groups— online or in person—we have a better chance of helping injustices and getting support for our frustrations of our political system. If a group is too daunting, we may find another with similar interests, perhaps taking risk to share our concerns and to support each other in the giving out. During my years of chronic illness, I had little energy for engaging in injustice or connecting to others. However, I met someone at a retreat, and we took a risk to make a friendship when we both were struggling with energy. We gave space for each other to tell our stories and encourage our activism in small ways, forming a blossoming relationship which continues to this day.

Creative ideas for this chapter

Exploring our subpersonalities

We sit in the quiet, giving space to connect with our breath, letting go of distractions. We give time to breathe, to connect to our senses, to open our listening ear.

We consider one of our current emotions or our mood, an attitude, or prominent trait; perhaps our anger or sadness has been stirred, or we have noticed a particular habit, or have been motivated to a certain action. We invite a part of ourselves to emerge; this takes an attitude of love, a quiet sitting, to allow an emergence through our imagination. We let an image emerge of this part, an image as a character, as an object, maybe something of nature like a tree or wind. Some of my examples include a snail, a shouty voice and an energetic lad.

We give this aspect space to emerge and notice the feeling it emanates. We may have a conversation with this part of us, and listen to what they are "saying" or imagine what they are doing. We may draw them out, and find out their needs. We take time to name them. Through exploration we can build a picture of what this part of us gives our personality and how we tend this part.

As we explore more of our aspects, we gain an overview of our inner life and the tussles that may be going on. We become more at home with this knowing, as our aspects converse with each other. This can be incorporated into the next suggested creative idea.[14]

Wisdom from our saints
This is a very helpful exercise, especially when we want to hear from our own Wisdom, perhaps in making a decision or listening to what happened in an event that has stirred our feelings.

We give space to breathe and prepare our minds to relax and let go of distractions. We bring to mind people from whom we would like to hear the voice of their Wisdom. These may be people dead or alive, in books and imaginary. We may also like to include other creatures and natural elements. We may surprise ourselves with who comes to mind, perhaps a child, a river, a wise teacher, or "unknown" (which one guest chose). We can also place around the table one or more of our subpersonalities that we have explored.

We imagine these characters around a circular table, making space for ourselves to join the circle. We state what we would like to hear from this gathering and take time to listen to each offering, whether verbal or sensory. Perhaps we draw this out and write out our findings.

This is an enlightening exercise of the Wisdom within, coming through in the different relationships that we have in our inner and outer worlds.[15]

We finish this chapter with the Pilgrim Prayer with its openness to learn from Wisdom through all different aspects.

Pilgrim Prayer

Teach me . . .
to ponder with the pilgrim;
to play with the piper;
to persevere with the pioneer.

To dance with the dervish;
to dare with the dreamer;
to declare with the daffodils.

To sing with the song-writer;
to smile with the sunshine;
to sigh with the sorrowful.

To run with the radical;
to re-member with the raging;
to rest with the retreatant.

To wonder with the wise;
to watch with the wounded;
to walk with the wretched.

To be with the battered;
to breathe with the beautiful;
to begin with the baby . . .

who will teach me . . . [16]

Notes

[1] Jan Berry, "We reach for a welcome", in Jan Berry and Andrew Pratt (eds) with Janet Eldred and Anne Sardeson, *Hymns of Hope and Healing* (London: Stainer & Bell, 2017), p. 2. © 2017 Stainer & Bell Ltd, 23 Gruneisen Road, London N3 1LS, www.stainer.co.uk. Used by permission. All rights reserved. Jan Berry worked in the Community of Holy Rood House for many years and arranged this hymn book through Holy Rood House.

[2] Roberto Assagioli, quoted in Piero Ferrucci, *What We May Be: Techniques for Psychological and Spiritual Growth through Psychosynthesis* (New York: Tarcher/Penguin, 2004), p. 48.

[3] Rowan Williams, *Being Human: Bodies, Minds, Persons* (London: SPCK, 2018), p. 40.

[4] Satish Kumar, Mahatma Gandhi's Philosophy of Love for All, <https://www.navdanya.org/latest-news-at-navdanya/701-mahatma-gandhis-philosophy-of-love-for-all>.

[5] 1 Corinthians 13:7.

[6] George Fox, founder of the Quakers, quoted in Harold Loukes, *Quaker Faith and Practice*, fifth edition (Oxford: Berforts Information Press, 2013), 2.23.

[7] Loukes, *Quaker Faith and Practice*, 2.23.

[8] Mother Julian of Norwich, *Revelations of Divine Love*, trs and eds Halcyon Backhouse and Rhona Pipe (London: Hodder & Stoughton, 1987), Chapter 48, p. 91.

[9] Alistair McIntosh, *Soil and Soul: People versus Corporate Power* (London: Aurum Press, an imprint of Quarto Publishing, 2004), p. 124.

[10] Poem created on a group retreat, *Poetry and Art from Holy Rood House: A Celebration of 25 Years 1993–2018* (independently published, 2019), p. 29.

[11] Carol Bialock (sufi poet), "The Future of Community", in *Coral Castles* (Portland, OR: Fernwood Press, 2019), p. 97.

[12] Quote from a guest, *Poetry and Art from Holy Rood House*, p. 4.

[13] From a talk by Margaret Barker at Continuing the Journey conference 2018, <https://continuingthejourney.com/conference-history/conference-history-2018-2>.

[14] Exercise adapted from Piero Ferrucci, *What We May Be*, p. 48.

[15] Exercise adapted from Tom Gordon, *A Need for Living: Signposts on the Journey of Life and Beyond* (Glasgow: Wild Goose Publications, 2001), p. 205.

[16] Elizabeth Baxter, *Holy Rood House Community Prayer* (independently published, 2017), p. 22.

CHAPTER 4

Wisdom calls through darkness

It is a darker time and yet I am coming alive. It is almost as
though the darkness is understanding my state of being; there is
a knowing in its depths. I am wrapped in its comfort.[1]

There is abundant life that thrives in darkness. Our own lives start in the
dark of the womb, seeds crack open in the dark earth, and many creatures
live in the darkness. In the northern hemisphere in the depth of winter,
we can have over twice as many hours of darkness as we do in the light
of summer. In this chapter, we explore what darkness can offer to the
emergence of Wisdom—the physical presence of darkness, as well as our
inner darkness of suffering—and what can stifle this process.

We often think of ourselves as people of the light and ignore the call of
darkness. We switch on the lights as soon as darkness falls and draw the
curtains to shut out the blackness outside. I started seeing the potential of
exploring what darkness offered throughout a chronic illness. Darkness
of the nights was a place where the felt sense of anxiety was exacerbated,
with night sweats and nightmares creating many restless hours. Over
many months, I tried to face this darkness, reviewing it as a quiet,
reflective space where I was not disturbed by others. I started to look at
my dreams and try and note how Wisdom emerged from them. I knew
that I could be in charge of these hours and become more empowered in
my dreams by facing up to the terrors of the night. Feeling so powerless
through my fragility, it felt good to realize that I could face some of my
fears and let Wisdom emerge.

Nights are now a place where I explore a different reflective space,
one with stillness where I feel uninhibited and able to stretch out into
darkness and to experience what it offers. If I am anxious about an issue,

I see this as restricting this offering; it is controlling my mind in a way that is unhelpful. I imagine opening out to dark space to listen to what else is around for me; to link to my body to soothe and wait for Wisdom's emergence:

> I love the dark hours of my being.
> My mind deepens into them.[2]

I am often nudged awake to reflect on a happening from the light of day, perhaps to learn and digest something, and not to miss Wisdom's insight from dark reflecting, which is very different from daytime reflections. When I am planning my organized events, the nights are often times when I manage to bring together what needs to be said. The creative brain can thrive in the night; the logical brain seems to need the light.

The blurring of boundaries in the darkness, the fears connected to the dark and the ruminations that occur in the quiet of the night, can make the nights a really difficult time. Many of our guests that come to Holy Rood House suffer from insomnia, although many sleep better in a safer space, away from home difficulties. Night-time can be a space when anxiety increases, and because this feels unpleasant, and increases our fears, we distract ourselves and push away darkness, refusing to dig deeper into its treasures. Some ideas of exploring darkness are included at the end of this chapter, many that we incorporate at Holy Rood House, which means we are rarely called out in the night to guests.

There was one night I was called by a guest suffering a night terror. The body reacts in the same way with nightmares as if it is going through the same thing in reality. Imagination or reality—the brain cannot distinguish. So the terrors felt from nightmares are acting out the same in the body. These are times in the night when we need reassurance and calming. For this guest, after we had done some deep, slow breathing together (and had a cup of tea), I showed her some acupressure points that are helpful in times of agitation. The body needs to feel safe, so saying reassuring words can also help: *I am safe, I am sitting on my chair, I can feel the floor under my feet*—words to ground and be where we are.

For us to open out to Wisdom in darkness, it is helpful for us to learn what the body does in panic, anxiety, stress or trauma and how to activate calming ways to reassure the body. If we feel more in control in our nights, we can learn to trust and open out to that inner Wisdom. The community has many study days on trauma, so we can access Wisdom and can be helpful, rather than catch the anxiety of the guest in question. If we can reverse the panic in our bodies by calming and grounding ourselves, we allow for the movement of Wisdom, opening to creative hope. With this guest we had some time exploring how anxiety works, and in the art room over the next few days, she explored her more vulnerable self, supported by her Wisdom self. She found after a couple of days her hands had become looser and she was able to connect to sketching again, drawing out a lovely flowing dancer and a Wisdom tree—the latter now framed at Holy Rood House.

There are times in our lives, such as with this guest, where it is beneficial to have help through our darkness. Many of our guests find the *knowing* about our community helpful in the nights that are bleaker. They may be on their own, yet they know that we are there—strengthening in spirit, and giving the hope needed. Sri Chinmoy, a spiritual teacher, talks about hope as the intuitive divinity in us. Hope can be a connection to our imagination, our life-force, a sense of seeing and drawing us on through life. We can imagine the help we need in the nights and empower ourselves through our intuitive selves:

> Life and hope are inseparable.
> Life is the body, and hope is the intuitive divinity in us.[3]

I have spilled out from the night times of rest, to connect to darkness when alert. When I walk in the dark, especially in the early morning, I can feel the freshness of the new day emerging and enjoy this sensory experience. The wildlife is less threatened by my presence; I have had a blackbird and a hedgehog on separate occasions come right up to my feet in the twilight. Watching the light fade into darkness is a lovely meditation. In these liminal times of morning and evening, I can connect to something within myself that is "recognized" in darkness. Recognized means "to know again, to perceive an identity with something formerly known or felt", and there is a welcoming within this dark spaciousness, a coming home to myself that feels connecting and joyful.

The coronavirus (Covid-19) pandemic was a time of chaos that hovered over the world—connecting us all with similar difficulties. During the initial months of the pandemic, I found myself using darkness for my reflecting. This was a sensory space to listen, to touch and sit with such a world catastrophe. The darkness gave me an outer spaciousness that held my inner spaciousness. I recognized this outer spaciousness from the Quaker worship meetings—where issues that felt too huge to face alone, could be sat with and held in love. Darkness became an understanding space, a space that seemed to know the depth of suffering, a space where I was reminded of that enveloping comfort. So darkness became the accompanier for me in my anxiety and perplexity.

In the fragility of our bodies during the pandemic times, the community explored a sense of opening out to something deeper within, a vulnerability that connected to an aspect of Wisdom which we termed the vulnerable Spirit. It is a Spirit that we knew from the hope we held and a way of being as community and we felt this vulnerable Spirit led us sensitively in these times, as in all times.

Suffering and darkness can expose our vulnerability. We often stop ourselves from feeling vulnerable as it is an uncomfortable sense and can bring up images of weakness, of not coping well. I accompanied a guest who had always been very competent and was seen by her friends as the capable one. When her physical health started deteriorating with a long-term condition, she found many of her friends were not supporting her; they were used to her managing. We explored the side of her that wept, the soft voice within that had to admit the struggle. She was able to listen to that vulnerable part of herself and learn what it would be like to state her needs, to be honest with her friends.

Henri Nouwen, a Dutch priest and theologian, explored vulnerability when recovering from a breakdown:

> As long as your vulnerable self does not feel welcomed by you, it keeps so distant that it cannot show you its true beauty and wisdom. When you become more childlike, it will no longer feel the need to dwell elsewhere. It will begin to look to you as home.
>
> Be patient. When you feel lonely, stay with your loneliness. Avoid the temptation to let your fearful self run off. Let it teach

you its wisdom; let it tell you that you can live instead of just surviving.[4]

Our vulnerable aspect opens us to beauty and love. Much of life is in the unknowing and it can take courage to experience our vulnerabilities, alongside our emotions. Sometimes when we name our vulnerability and what emotion, health state or situation is connecting to this, we can allow ourselves to find the nurturing voice within to enable a support for our vulnerabilities, imagining this voice connected to Love. One guest, in her painful journey, was able to name her lostness, with a sense of disorientation and lack of clear path. This acknowledgement helped her to explore her vulnerable side and the creative opportunities that being lost brought to her. There was a part of her that now understood what was going on. It can be our vulnerability that can be the healer in our journeys, a part of us that knows difficulty and fragility, opening us to a deeper intuitive divinity.

Darkness gives us experience of chaos and of deep mystery. Many of us want a clear path, and darkness gives us the experience of no path, of being within an unclear environment. In the Genesis myth of creation, darkness covered the earth as a unitive presence, a chaotic, violent movement, the Hebrew word *choshekh* meaning a force to liberate itself. Out of this imbalance and chaos came an enlightened presence—not the light of daylight, this initial light was the start of bringing life to the earth, an energy that created: Hokhmah/Sophia as the creative process:

> In the beginning when God created the heavens and the earth, the earth was a formless void and darkness covered the face of the deep, while a wind from God swept over the face of the waters. Then God said, "Let there be light"; and there was light. And God saw that the light was good; and God separated the light from the darkness. God called the light Day, and the darkness Night. And there was evening and there was morning, the first day.[5]

Meister Eckhart explored the Genesis sense of void or nothingness, and referred to this emptiness that we can also encounter within us.

He speculated that nothingness (*ayin* in Hebrew) and Wisdom travel together:

> The beginning of existence is the secret concealed point, primordial wisdom, the secret conceptual point. That which abides in thought yet cannot be grasped is called wisdom: Hokhmah.[6]

This way of travelling has no maps, a way of dark exploring, connected to Wisdom that Meister Eckhart described as waiting for what will come and what will be.

So darkness offers a waiting space, where in the potential of the now there may be movement, ideas, a breaking through. A sense of purpose can come out of the expansion of the moment, and there is much learning for us to do, to be able to be in the present moment, without our heads being in the past or future. Etty Hillesum, in her struggles through the Second World War as a Jew, describes her way out of suffering:

> This, too, is one of my latest achievements: the realization that every moment gives birth to a new moment, full of fresh potential, and sometimes like an unexpected present. And that one must not cling to moments of malaise and prolong them needlessly, because in so doing one may prevent the birth of a richer moment. Life courses through one as a constant current in a great series of moments, each having its own place in the day.[7]

It often takes suffering for us to listen outside of our own egos; we start searching for answers, for ways out, for a healing route. Suffering takes us into a liminal space where we are out of control and thrown into the chaos of the darkness. It is this space that mirrors the mystery to which Wisdom's way is so connected.

I have been accompanying a guest on her deeply traumatic journey after the tragic death of her partner. Through this period of grief, nightmares, lack of direction and howling, she started painting. Glimpses of colour began appearing out of the initial blackness and this transition gave her a felt sense of something hopeful. We were able to name a sense of connection which seemed to fit the name of "the ground of being". This ground of all being—a term that the Buddhist Thich Nhat Hanh and the theologian Paul Tillich utilize—reflected the rock bottom place in which she groped, and now seemed to be giving her a sense of comfort, of hope and of direction. Here in the muddy mire was emerging glimpses of a way through her pain.

The term "the ground of being" I find a helpful one when going through suffering. I think of foundation, the bedrock, the solidity of the earth, a sense of grounding, that can help our body feel more held as we explore the darkness. Hildegard referred to Mary, mother of Jesus, as the ground of being, with her expression of love and nurturing and her representation of Mother Earth.[8] In this hidden darkness there is often fertile ground where Wisdom cracks the seeds of potential. Edith Stein, in a prayer that starts "I know myself held in peace and security", encapsulates this sense of connection within darkness with her finishing lines:

> Hence in my being I meet another Being who is not mine but the support and ground of my unsupported and groundless being.[9]

Some of us will be more familiar with this ungrounded, vulnerable side, activated when we are anxious, panicky and have concerns and fears that often take over our thinking and being. When we are immersed in this aspect, we can remind ourselves of other aspects of ourselves, especially the part of us that is rooted, grounded, connected to the earth and links to that spark of life. Wisdom brings the gifts of the earth, the miracle of human life, the love of others, the goodness of being, out of this rootedness. There is an exercise that I did with many guests during these pandemic times (see end of chapter) that helpfully explores how the grounded part of us can support our overwhelmed, reactive part.

Holy Rood House has a large basement—always in darkness apart from the light turned on with visits. One day I descended the stairs, and as I searched for an item, I noticed a strange package. In a rectangular box, wrapped with Christmas paper, a bud was escaping through the packaging. This was an Amaryllis bulb, uncollected as a present for a member of staff on our yearly secret Santa. This Amaryllis (which apparently symbolizes determination and love) had no water and only darkness, and yet it contained a yearning for the light, to reach its created potential. It needed to live, and somehow it grew in this restricted environment.

In times of challenge, we often want to try and control our environment, maybe building protective structures around our fragile selves. Sometimes these structures are needed to help defend us in times of fear, abuse, illness and suffering. When we are able to listen to the nurturing voice of Wisdom this can help us to assess whether these structures still need to be in place, or whether they are affecting our life-force that urges us towards our potential.

One guest's exploring illustrates this concept. She came to Holy Rood House and reflected on three images about herself. One was of water bubbling up from a fountain within, and another was of a brick wall completely surrounding her—four walls, like a prison. The third image was of a light behind the wall. In her past, she had suffered from ME or Chronic Fatigue Syndrome and felt the need of those walls for inner protection at a very difficult time in her life. We went slowly and with care with this image. The guest offered a conversation with the walls, being encouraged to use a nurturing voice, a voice connected to love. Out of the conversing with the image came a clarity of what the walls needed and how they might be changed. A further conversation took time to thank the walls for doing what they needed to, with an explaining of what the guest wanted now. She decided a gentle approach would be to start taking out the odd brick. This would represent her doing something that wasn't controlled, perhaps doing something spontaneously, saying "yes" to something, as she realized that the brick wall was about her wanting to control life. She knew that with each brick taken out of the wall the light would shine through—light that she knew was within her. The image of the water was reflecting aspects of messiness and chaos which were a struggle for her. Further conversation was had with the chaotic, messy fountain that she related to the Spirit within which had a reassuring voice connecting her to safety.

Wisdom arises through the symbolic as we find symbols that connect to us through our images, dreams and our noticings. These reflections of aspects of ourselves need to be held in love and gently explored, so Wisdom's gift of understanding and her creative energy can emerge.

There are many symbols that can help us connect to darkness. China Galland writes about the Black Madonna, which is a symbol that has been venerated for centuries in the great cathedrals around the world. She explains that Madonna (from the Italian "my lady") represents Mary, the mother of Christ, and she symbolizes healing (remembering the reference to the ground of being). There could be many reasons for her colour: maybe she is psyche's shadow, maybe she has absorbed so much suffering. China Galland's theory is that she is dark because she is all colours and has absorbed all colours. The Black Madonnas come from traditions in which black symbolizes Wisdom. The Dark Mother rises by healing waters, streams, rivers, and deltas. In some places, she is associated with storms, lightning, and thunder:

> The image of the Black Madonna, the Dark Mother, is arising in the human psyche now because we need her. Images of the sacred are vessels, containers. They function as portals, doorways, porous membranes through which the unseen world can pour. She is rising to remind us that what we call darkness is invisible light. That 90% of what is, is invisible. That darkness matters, is to be valued, treasured.[10]

The Black Madonna is one of many divine feminine figures that represents fierce compassion with fierceness as an anger that comes from love, and kindness incorporated within this healing image.

We are far more comfortable when we are feeling stable and calm. We tend to forget that our bodies are designed to go through different seasons. We have times of waiting, of grief and loss, of blossoming and being fruitful, of barrenness, and hardship. We want to focus on the times of stability and knowing where we are going. The times when we feel lost, uncertain, in chaos, are opportunities that are needed for learning and exploring. For example, with grief, we need a period of instability, of lostness, to take apart the pattern or jigsaw that has been formed with the person we grieve. In the chaotic times, there needs to be space for a new jigsaw to be formed, to reintegrate that person in a different way. This can only be done through a very slow process of letting go and getting the help we need to hear our own Wisdom.

I found an interesting process went on for me with grieving for my father. Eighteen months before he died this is what I wrote in my journal:

> A beautiful thing happened to me last night. From the reminiscence treasure chest, Wisdom let escape an old song "Underneath the Spreading Chestnut Tree". As it came I had an "oh wow" moment. It seemed special, deep in the night. It feels like this song, one heard played by my father in my childhood, has opened the way for other treasures to come through. I feel I can trust the grief journey if these pearls are going to come through in the darkest night.

I had the benefit of time (which I realize may not often be given), and throughout the 18 months had reflective and comforting glimpses from my spaciousness. By the time my dad did die, I was able to cope better with the grief process. I went with the flow of my body's early morning awakenings and used these times for reflection, journaling, walks and creating. A couple of years on, on the eve of what would have been Dad's birthday, I had a lovely dream of my father tenderly giving me a brief kiss. It was a treasured moment, charming, intimate and loving. This was the same week that I was accompanying the guest that had the night terror. The knowing of comfort from my own Wisdom was an enabler in my helping of this person in the night.

Over the months I felt that this grief journey had opened another part of me—somehow expanded myself. It was a part of me that I felt had awakened, one that I had not had access to before this death.

The depth of night has become an exploration of grief for another member of our community. His grief journey formed into a time of reflection and prayer, within his garden, from the hours of two to three in the morning—a space where most streetlights are off and there is little traffic noise. He describes an accentuated hearing and feeling sense, such as the wisps of wind on his face—not realized in the light. In the night sky the stars evoke a depth of space and a sense of looking into history; something seen, made millions of years ago. In the dark depths,

he experiences a sense of timelessness, of time becoming flexible—
where past, present and future cease to be the usual sequential events
and instead fold into each other in the present moment. In this sensory
space, Wisdom is essence, and prayer flows with this essence, aiding a
conversational pattern with the people in his thoughts. This is his vigil, of
watching in the time of suffering. He finds the night creatures help keep
that vigil, especially the owl. He takes into this darkness the awareness
that according to our Christian story Jesus did much of his personal
praying in the early hours of darkness before dawn. Jesus was also born in
the dark, betrayed in the dark, crucified in the dark and was resurrected
in the dark.

> Joyful is the dark
> Spirit of the deep,
> winging wildly o'er the world's creation,
> silken sheen of midnight,
> plumage black and bright,
> swooping with the beauty of a raven.[11]

The seasons of nature take us through different levels of darkness,
reflecting the seasons of our own bodies. Winter gives those of us in the
northern hemisphere increased darkness which can enable more rest and
reflection. There may be projects—perhaps creative ventures—that can
be carried out in the winter months for which we may be able to prepare,
and to which we may look forward. I have learnt to appreciate the winter,
with its more accessible offerings of dark explorings, especially linked to
the moon and night sky and to the glimpses of the resident tawny owls.

The darkness of winter

> In you I am most alive
> held by your sinewy touch
> enveloped in your merging
> all boundaries broken

I watch your coming
darkness outspreading
blackbirds sounding your arrival
calling others to dark happenings

I expand into you
my antennae searching
for what you bring forth
You hear my heartbeat rhythms
and hold my yearnings in your embrace

Purple stars, dense shadows
call me to adventure
yet your fertile soil grounds me
and captures creative seeds

I feel my belonging
through your immensity
smell the comfort of your womb
which ripens my prayer into being[12]

After one of the online creative journaling events which took place in September, one guest mentioned that autumn was always a challenging time for her as she finds change difficult and knows that autumn leads to the darkness of winter. During the creative time we explored the autumn equinox, a time in the year around 22 September where there is roughly 12 hours of darkness and 12 hours of light all over the world. The symbol of this is the double spiral—with a line that moves from the outer bounty of the summer, into the inward reflection of winter, and outwards again. Exploring this movement, we looked at what might be gestating within us, getting ready to give birth through the darkness. The guest was more hopeful, having taken some creative time exploring the topic, that she would be open to new experiences that this time of year offered.

Rituals can be a way of preparing and celebrating darkness. They tap into the sensory language and ancient ways where Wisdom thrives. Rituals can be a way of re-membering who we are and how we belong, in the various transitions through life. The ritual acknowledges the occasion, revering its connection with the season, cosmos or event that has been happening throughout the generations. These can be marked with chants, candle lighting, prayers, poems, circle dancing, body movements and other creative expressions. Throughout the year at Holy Rood House, we connect to seasonal aspects of darkness such as the solstices in December and June and the equinoxes in March and September. The winter solstice occurs at the darkest point of the year—three days around 22 December (northern hemisphere), where the sun appears to stand still, rising and setting in the same place for three days, whilst it turns to go the other direction. We also connect to the darkness and waiting through the periods of Advent—four weeks before Christmas—and Lent—six weeks before Easter.

Ideas for opening to Wisdom in darkness

Darkness can offer a recovery space, a spacious, intimate place where the felt sense of Wisdom can arise, an accompanier through our suffering. As we will all have our own uncertainties about darkness, we go gently in our exploring. We may prefer to have accompaniment—by connecting to a good friend, a counsellor or spiritual accompanier who can support us as we listen to the process of Wisdom in the dark. We may like to pick one of these ideas to start our exploring.

We may like to watch in the morning or the evening, the light appearing or disappearing, and make this a stilling practice for ourselves. We are "being with" whatever is going on for us in this "thin" space. As we watch and listen, we open to this liminal space and its offering.

If we have a quiet space, we may like to be in a darkened room with the light of a candle. This is a much softer light than electricity, with a sense of being able to see the darkness through this gentle light. We can notice how the eyes adjust to gradually distinguish more shapes. We could try gentle movements in darker spaces and might also like to get creative and use clay, writing, drawing, painting in the darkness, aware of our heightened senses in this creative space.

The evening can be a time of reflection as the day ends. We can sit with what has gone on in the day and notice what has stirred, what small things have happened, where the creative energy has been. Evenings can also be preparation time for our opening to Wisdom in the night. We may want some winding down activities that will help us to shake off the difficulties of the day and open our creative brain. Screen time, although distracting, can be a stimulant, so we may experiment with stretches, music, meditation, relaxing with light reading. The body takes to routine and sometimes just a few minutes can help settle.

We can feel more vulnerable in letting go, when opening to Wisdom in the dark. We may like to keep grounded by reminding ourselves of our connection to Love, of our connection to the earth, of our trusting the potential of darkness. We can reflect on what we are thankful for, on beauty, on what has happened recently that has been helpful. Some people appreciate having a phrase to focus on and there are many quotes in this book for longer reflection.

As we go into sleep, we can be expectant to what might emerge as we ask Wisdom to be an accompanier to our night. We can let the bed support us and feel snug under covers. If there are times when we are awake, we can give this time over to opening to Wisdom, perhaps conversing with darkness, and asking for a way through the night. We might want a notebook by our bed for recording dreams and other helpful thoughts.

There is an important space as we awaken that the poet David Whyte captures:

> In that first hardly noticed moment in which you wake, /there
> is a small opening into the new day /which closes the moment
> you begin your plans.[13]

As we come to, bleary eyed, there is a space for capturing any creative energy gathered in the darkness, to spark new beginning. Each morning we are offered a fresh start, and this is a precious space for capturing Wisdom.

Darkness is about slowing down, listening, and experiencing a different perspective. Darkness reflects our experiences of not having a path, of having to sit with the "what is". These are waiting times, and it might be that we have darkness as part of a weekly ritual: perhaps having time in a darker room to listen to the Wisdom of that week, to reflect and be, waiting for our intuition to help us through. This can be a healing space, an understanding space to sit with the confusion of the world and hold the pain of our loved ones.

We may like to experience darkness outside. Most of our built-up places will be affected by light pollution, although there may be times when we can see some of the stars. The moon can be tracked, and we may like to notice the waxing and waning of the moon, another symbol of Wisdom.

We could make our own ritual for darkness, finding chants, poems, prayers and creative expressions for certain times of the year such as Advent, Lent and going into the winter. Here is one ritual that we do at Holy Rood House connecting to the seasons that reflect the rhythm of the natural world as well as the different aspects of ourselves.

Calling the directions—for healing and transformation of the world[14]

This is a blessing ritual that we often do in our healing garden. It connects with the four main compass points and the fundamental harmony of all being. We acknowledge all aspects of these directions within us and connect to our own active role in the creation of harmony out of chaos. We may like to stand, facing each direction for a few minutes' reflection and quiet, perhaps holding our hands out in a receiving gesture with each direction, to receive blessing. We make it our own, ignoring anything that is unhelpful to us and letting our reflections be a blessing.

EAST—Sunrise, the season of spring
The start of a new day, connecting to new life. The colour is red connecting to the sunrise. We connect to the vitality, hope and strength of the sun with its light and heat as the source of life for all creation. The element is air, and we connect to our breath, aware of our in-breath and out-breath. We are aware of the temperature of the air on our skin, and if we are outside, we feel the wind, or we open a window to feel the breeze.

We connect to the young generation, the energy and vitality of youth within us. We receive energy for our lives and the blessings from the east.

WEST—Sunset, the season of autumn

The end of the day—evening time, connecting to a reflective time and the liminal space of getting dark. The colour is black, connecting to gestation in life, hibernation, and storing up of resources. We reflect on what is gestating within us, and within the earth. The element is water, and we reflect on the flow and way of water. Water is the main component in most of our body cells and our first few months of life are in a watery womb. We connect to expectancy of what will arise from our reflection and gestations. The west links into the masculine energy within us all, and we remember helpful males in our lives. We imagine letting go, shown by the season of autumn, and open to the blessing of the west.

NORTH—Night, the season of winter

Our resting space, often in the darkness. We connect to the potential of what emerges from darkness. We link to the element of the earth with the grounding it offers. We feel the earth under our feet and its potential energy. We reflect on what happens in the earth in the winter—its holding, storing and allowing; bulbs resting in this space getting ready for the energy of spring. The colour is white, representing cold, ice and purity. The north links us to the elderly and the Wisdom of those in their older life. We remember death and the ancestors that gave us life. We think of the wise people in our lives. We receive the blessing of rest, and strength and Wisdom to make new beginnings, to bring about reconciliation.

SOUTH—Noon, the season of summer

The fullness of the day, with the sun at its highest. We connect to flourishing, to fruitfulness, to new life and abundance. We ask for compassion in our hearts to melt any iciness or fear. We let love be our highest quality and desire. The element is fire, and we appreciate the heat of the sun, and we feel the warmth that energy brings to our body. We connect to the energy of the feminine and remember women who have had a positive influence on our lives. The colour is yellow linking to sunshine, creativity and happiness. We receive the blessings of the south of peace, joy and fulfilment.

THE CENTRE—where all the directions meet

We face the centre, imagining a place where all the directions meet. The colours are blue (sky) and green (earth), representing the union of the earthly and the spiritual; of humanity and divine. We reflect on the Spirit of Oneness connecting all directions, giving a sense of belonging and representing the oneness of all creation. We receive the blessing of the new reality of harmony and grace that emerges through this centre.

Creative ideas for this chapter

Exploring our vulnerable side and our grounded side

We start with a blank sheet of paper, A4 or larger, with the longer side at the top. We draw a line down the middle, so the paper is in two halves. One side of the paper is for exploring our grounded side. This is the part of us that is stable, wise and enlightened. There is a knowing in this part of light, hope and love. This part links into the miracle of life, the wonder of the earth and the connection with others. There is a sense of belonging, perhaps a connection with faith.

The other side of the paper is for exploring our vulnerable aspect. The part of us that is anxious, wobbly, that wants to run away from ourself. It is an uncomfortable part and can be hard to handle.

We try and do this swiftly, not getting caught up in the emotions, just letting shapes, colours and words come onto the paper.

We note how these are both aspects of ourselves and we may imagine a conversation between the two parts. This can be done in our imagination or with writing—perhaps using a different colour for each side of the paper.

How do we become aware of these different areas within us?

How does our grounded side support our vulnerable side?

Connecting to the earth in dark times

This exercise imagines the soil and all that it offers in the darkness. We explore a sense of fertile ground within ourselves and what happens when our difficulties meet this space. We may like to have some soil in a bowl for this exercise.

We begin with our breathing, noting our breathing out and our breathing in, slowing and deepening our inhale and exhale. We feel our feet on the ground and connect to the solidness of the earth. We imagine the bedrock underneath our feet and connect to the security that it offers. We imagine our in-breath travelling down our body and into our feet, and as we breathe out, we imagine the breath bringing up the energy of the earth through our body and out into the air.

We are made of the same elements as the soil. We connect to all that the soil offers, to feel the texture, and reflect on all it contains—minerals, organic matter and helpful bacteria. The soil has all it needs to break open seeds in its darkness and release the potential of the seed.

We place our hands on our pelvis area, around our guts. We breathe into this area and imagine the soil, the earth of our being, at our core, at the depth of our being. This is a fertile, dark area, full of the richness we need for our life. Like the earth, it is full of minerals, and healthy microbes. Perhaps we imagine what this looks like.

We bring into this imagining any difficult emotions that may be around for us, perhaps our despair. We imagine one of these as a seed that we let fall into this ground of our being. So our seed of despair, or our seed of longing, of lostness, of grief perhaps, falls into this fertile earth and is held. There may be more than one seed. The seeds have to lie in this depth, to be held, to be broken open, to release their potential. We sit and wait, whilst our ground of being, connected to love, holds our seeds in the darkness.

As the seeds break open, they release their potential. We wait to see what happens to our seeds. We spend time now with this image. We may want to converse with the ground of our being and ask a question. We may listen to hear the answer.

We may want to write something down after we have had some time with this exercise.

One guest who did this exercise was recovering from Covid. She said she had been feeling like a dried-out husk, and this exercise showed her there is potential in her and life to come.

Prayer for the night

Strong and lovely one,
gather up our weariness;
free up our heaviness.

As the night draws in
the Spirit wafts her way through the shadows
integrating light and darkness;
beaming her presence;

***opening up our possibilities
for tomorrow.***[15]

Notes

[1] Winter Journal writings.

[2] Rainer Maria Rilke, *Rilke's Book of Hours: Love Poems to God*, trs and eds Anita Barrows and Joanna Macy (New York: Riverhead Books, 1997), I,5 . <https://dailypoetry.me/rilke/the-dark-hours-of-my-being/>.

[3] <https://www.poetseers.org/sri-chinmoy/sri-chinmoy-quotes/quotes-hope/>.

[4] Henri Nouwen, *The Inner Voice of Love* (London: Darton, Longman & Todd, 1997), p. 41.

[5] Genesis 1:1–5 (adapted).

[6] Matthew Fox, *Meister Eckhart: A Mystic Warrior for our Times* (Novato, CA: New World Library, 2014), p. 134.

[7] Etty Hillesum, *Etty: The Letters and Diaries of Etty Hillesum 1941–1943*, ed. Klaus A. D. Smelik, tr. Arnold J. Pomerans (Grand Rapids, MI: Eerdmans Publishing Co., 2002), p. 211.

[8] Fox, *Meister Eckhart*, p. 46.

9   Edith Stein, prayer in James McCaffrey, *The Fire of Love: Praying with Thérèse of Lisieux* (Norwich: Canterbury Press, 1998), p. 57.

10 China Galland, *The Bond between Women: A Journey to Fierce Compassion* (New York: Riverhead Books, 1998), p. 187.

11 Brian Wren, "Joyful is the Dark", © 1989 Stainer & Bell Ltd, 23 Gruneisen Road, London N3 1LS, www.stainer.co.uk. Used by permission. All rights reserved.

12 Author, 2019, previously unpublished.

13 David Whyte, "What to Remember When Waking", from *River Flow: New and Selected Poems* (Langley, NJ: Many Rivers Press, 2012).

14 Based on Capacitar exercise from a training course. Re-written.

15 Elizabeth Baxter, *Holy Rood House Community Prayer* (independently published, 2017), p. 186.

CHAPTER 5

Wisdom calls through the Earth

Can you find out the deep things of God?
But ask the animals, and they will teach you;
the birds of the air, and they will tell you;
ask the plants of the earth, and they will teach you;
and the fish of the sea will declare to you.

Job 11:7; 12:7–8

Homo sapiens have only been around for five to seven million years of the 13.8 billion years of the existence of the universe. Our bodies have evolved from the same elements as the earth—water, carbon and hydrogen, with the addition of microscopic organisms such as bacteria, fungi and viruses, most of which live in our gut, making over half of our body other-than-human.[1] Each of us is an environment; we are wild beings, containing the ancient ways of the earth.

From a toddler, my granddaughter welcomed the plants and trees in her neighbourhood. She would tenderly touch a leaf, say "hello" when she could speak, or wave a farewell to what she knew were her associates in her world. We are born knowing that we belong, that the trees and birds are our friends, and in this chapter we will consider our connection with the earth, our belonging and Wisdom's relational way that leads to a wider unity.

My own eco-story includes many walks in all weathers as a child and the excitement of early morning walks on holiday with my father and siblings (never understanding why my mother would want to miss these excursions and stay in bed!). My father also gave us small sections of the garden to tend and grow flower seeds, and I learnt from observing his growing of fruit and vegetables. I have always enjoyed walking, bird watching and holidaying in beautiful countryside.

The environment of Holy Rood House, set within the ancient county of North Yorkshire, sandwiched on a fairly level plain between the North York Moors and the Yorkshire Dales, has expanded my earth-flourishings. The big skies, easy access to walks, and the small river running a field's walk away, free me to breathe and reflect. My early morning wanderings bring sensations, some of which I will not forget, such as the excitement and intimacy of lying on a dark frosty earth, with a star-filled sky, accompanied by the tawny owl's hooting. On another occasion, three of our community, as part of a 24-hour musical fundraising marathon, walked down to the river in twilight, woolly-hatted, singing and ringing bells to bring in the dawn and give blessing for the earth.

I am amazed at the miracles of the earth's growing and tending. Our compost, which accepts the kitchen peelings and goat manure, enables our garden fruit and vegetables to flourish. The wildlife enriches the environment, and we have guests who record the birdsong as a reminder of their sensed experience for when they are home.

For us to hear the subtle Wisdom of the earth, we may need to assess our relationship with the earth. Our identity is influenced at a deep pre-verbal level by our early experiences in nature and the cultural perspective of those around us. Many children are not given the opportunity to play in mud, climb trees, shout into the wind, camp out under the stars. Some guests come to us cut off from their senses and not engaging with nature, either from circumstance, or more often through trauma and anxiety; they miss the sense of grounding and balance that comes from our connection to the earth. One important feature within each bedroom and around the house is having seasonal flowers—bringing something of the garden into the house in a way that encourages beauty, delight and a connection to the seasons. Our pets are also helpful for guests to build a connection. Our wellbeing and creative sessions, garden days and Chapel spaces encourage us all to open to our senses and explore our own bodies in connection to nature and the processes of the seasons.

On one occasion, a guest walked out of a wellbeing session, very upset, and I found her weeping in the garden. After sitting with her, I gently encouraged her to the room where we had already booked some time together. On the way, through her tears, she noticed a solitary tree across the road, framed by the entrance to the driveway. The noticing stopped her, and she wanted to tell me of what she saw. I asked her what the tree was saying to her, and she spoke a few sentences about this tree: something of the fresh greenness, of standing on its own, of resilience and the tree being and doing what came naturally. We talked about this tree—the spaciousness around it and how it travelled through the seasons. The wellbeing group that she had found difficult had been offering a connection to a safe space within, held in love. She did not feel held in love and yet, her listening to the tree had shown her something of an offering of love that brought her hope.

To explore something of this connection to the earth and the movement of Wisdom I will introduce four different levels, or perspectives, which are ways of seeing the world through different realities or ways of experience. Each of these realities offers a way of connection to the earth, and although we move in and out of these perspectives, we might want to bring in ways to become more aware of these levels.[2]

Perspective 1 is ordinary reality or the objective world. I see everything as separate—there are the trees, the river, the field. The environment is there for me as a human, to influence in whatever way I wish. From this stance, I can see an overview of the environment, so I might want to plan what I do with the land—I might build on it, or create a garden. I could also decide not to engage with the environment.

I may go outside, enjoy a walk, although I may be still mulling over things in my head, so not noticing much around me.

Taking one field in this example, I may note its size, and what is going on in that field. I might enjoy my senses and the wildlife in this field—as just ordinary experiences.

To deepen this perspective, leading us to further levels, we bring in the sense of wonder. There are many instances in the natural world that awaken our wonder; the sunsets, birdsong, sculptural trees, glimpses of wildlife moments. We may get a feeling of amazement, admiration, joy, surprise. Children are good at wonder—looking and wanting to share their finds. Wonder is irrational, bypassing our rational brain and opening to our deep body-knowing.

Many uplifting conversations are experienced in our community on the wonder of seeing a merlin come to feed at the pond, meeting a hedgehog on an early walk, finding some hidden crocuses, seeing seven butterflies flying together, and hearing mating frogs laying masses of frogspawn in our pond! In February, we cut some of the aconites to float in a bowl of water, showing their yellow flowers opening over their thin green leaves, like mini waterlilies. Many admire the beauty of this simple act and feel uplifted, opening a way to receive and connect to the energy of the earth. As we open to the wonder and power of nature we tune in to Wisdom, *the breath of life from underneath, the Sense behind all senses, the one within that grasps meaning out of the bewildering swirl of existence.*[3]

Perspective 2 connects to a personal level as the subjective world. I know I am part of something bigger. Wonder opens me to awe, which might give me insight to a greater awareness. As I stand in the field, I am more aware of the interdependence of the natural world, of the way the rain enriches the earth, of growth, of the needs of the wildlife. I am part of this connection.

When I walk, I connect to my senses so I can be in my body and open to my deep body-knowing. I want to connect to what is drawing my attention. I might dive off into the trees as I notice something away from the path. What I notice I may bring into relationship with myself. I might stop with the crow as she caws and caw back, finding a dialogue. I go to the river after a week away and say to the river "I missed you". As I experience eye to eye contact with a tawny owl one early morning, I learn of the special memories that can build up through wild relationships.

I feel my emotions which might be peace, happiness, excitement. I experience the seasons, often linking the season to what is going on in my own body. I am aware that everything is connected, that everything is part of a cycle and in transition. I am perhaps aware of the energy of my own body as I feel the energy of the earth.

I try and refer to the plants and wildlife as beings, not as "its", maybe learning their names, or making my own name, as I know that we all belong together in this world.

As we go deeper into this perspective of awareness, of being part of a greater whole, we may find ourselves in a movement that draws us to explore. On a retreat one year, I had this sense of being on the cusp of something deep that was being revealed to me through nature. I was unmoved with the chaplain's offerings in this retreat, and whilst others were at morning prayer, I went into the grounds on the search for something that drew me, that wanted a connection with me. I found a particular rock and spent time with my senses, enjoying the texture, noticing what inhabited the rock and how the rock inhabited the environment. I would feel excitement visiting this rock again. The same feelings emerged with a felled tree that needed my time and examination; these sacred meetings felt precious:

> There is a deep, deep kinship in us, beneath the outer layers of the
> neocortex or what we learned at school. There is a deep wisdom,
> a bondedness with our creation, and an ingenuity far beyond
> what we think we have.[4]

Perspective 3 takes us to the symbolic world or a way of imagining. I let the creatures and living things inform me. I see that everything is part of a pattern, and exists in relationship. I explore a perspective that is not human. In my field, I might sit by a tree and allow the tree's Wisdom to infiltrate. I imagine what it is like to be the tree. I imagine myself with roots in the ground, sap rising as energy and breathing deep. I link what I see and sense to my own experience; perhaps the bird flying overhead reminds me of freedom, the last leaf on the tree to a sense of hope. I am moved by these enlightenings. I see all things as a reflection of myself, as informers of getting to know myself. I might have a sit space where I just am, getting to know my environment and what it has to give to me. I experience the seasons and explore the patterns and seasons in my own life. I am able to bring the big areas of exploration such as life, death, love and suffering into the environment to let it inform.

During the coronavirus (Covid-19) pandemic, I imagined a creature that could help me through; a pink fiery dragon that I named Hild (meaning "battle" I later established). This helped me with a concept of flying *over*, with an image of being up in the sky, where I could see from above an overall perspective on issues.

The imagination can be a wonderful tool in changing the perspective and enabling a connection to earth, the sky and all creation.

Perspective 4 brings us into a oneness in the holistic world. In the field, I experience myself *as* the field. I can feel the sun and the wind. I experience the environment as a oneness with myself. There is no sense of distinction between myself and the creation with which I identify. I am linked to the Cosmos, with a greater perspective. I might have this perspective as glimpses; a fleeting sense of unity or holding within a wider unity. I might experience this unity as I catch the eye of the tawny owl, or lie on the earth.

In this perspective, I am linked to the primitive, to my ancestors and my wild self, which is beautifully illustrated by the following quote:

> You know, there's a place we all inhabit, but we don't much think about it, we're scarcely conscious of it, and it lasts for less than a minute a day. It's in the morning, for most of us, it's that time, those few seconds when we're coming out of sleep but we're not really awake yet. For those few seconds we're something more primitive than what we are about to become. We have just slept the sleep of our most distant ancestors, and something of them and their world still clings to us. For those few moments we are unformed, uncivilized. We are not the people we know as ourselves, but creatures more in tune with a tree than a keyboard. We are untitled, unnamed, natural, suspended between was and will be, the tadpole before the frog, the worm before the butterfly. We are, for a few brief moments, anything and everything we could be.[5]

My experiences bring me into a sense of belonging, my core self as a oneness with the greater universe; my "I am" as a oneness with a greater "I am".

I was accompanying one guest who had an image of cowering in a dark tunnel; a grim, echoey place that had been built around her over the last 18 months. Her God was outside of the tunnel, and she felt the need to stand and shout. The next day she was awake early and watched the sunrise. Something happened in that moment of linking to this beautiful happening. During our time together, she spoke of the mystery of God coming through the cracks in the bricks of the tunnel, and the awareness of something hopeful coming into her grimness which was helping her to get to her feet.

As we try to express and articulate these glimpses of the whole of which we belong, we begin to appreciate ourselves within the natural environment and what gifts we are offered. I now have increased awareness of the effect that I have within the natural environment that might be voiced by birds and rustling trees that I walk by. I visited an ancient wood at one time, one of three Neolithic henges, thought to have ceremonial importance.[6] As soon as I walked into this circular structure, a short shower of rain shook all the leaves of the trees, just for a few seconds of my entry. I was the only person in the henge at that time, and I felt the trees were giving me a welcoming applause. Our being in the world causes a stir; we are noticed, we belong.

I am a mere beginner on this journey of exploring these perspectives, especially Perspective 4 that is highlighted by indigenous peoples all over the world: a way of living as one, with our deep knowing and the deep Wisdom of the earth.

We can be very daunted with the natural world. It can bring up innate fears when there are thunderstorms, noises in the dark and just the sheer size of the "outside". We have many guests who keep themselves "inside" in what they feel might be a safer space. Alongside these fears, we also experience anxiety as to what is happening with the earth, being upset with the reporting on the news, feeling helplessness with dominant companies not complying with reducing carbon emissions, and out of our depth with our contribution to caring for the planet. The following are some pointers of earthy Wisdom and how the way of Wisdom can help us to explore and expand the different perspectives with a way to care for ourselves and the natural world.

Connecting to the natural world

Indigenous people have learnt their healing and Wisdom from communications of the plants and animals in the natural world. The word "natural" stems from the Anglo-Saxon word *gecynd* which encompasses the wild nature of all beings as well as our quality derived from birth.

This word is feminine, and the meaning encompasses kindness; what is natural is wild as well as kind. Spending time in the natural world, connecting to what we are drawn to and listening to the connection within us, may lead us on a journey where nature with its kindness and wildness will inform, heal and transform.

> If we surrendered
> to earth's intelligence
> we could rise up rooted, like trees.[7]

The language of the earth is non-verbal, like the language of the body, so we need to find a way to relate to the earth, so that the earth can reassure us of her way of transformation and continuing existence. As well as opening to our senses we may need a different way of seeing, or being, to explore this connection. The writer and poet Rainer Maria Rilke used the term "inseeing" to describe an emotional connection to our observing; a sense of using our eyes *and* our feelings.[8] We also need to quieten or let go of our thoughts and what I call the chuntering brain, so we can focus on sensing the movement of Wisdom from what we notice. I sometimes find that what I notice can bring clarity to what is in my quietened thoughts—some treasure from the present moment.

There will be reciprocal caring as we find times of connecting with our feet and body on the earth, letting the earth energize and care for us. Having our hands in the soil, especially soil with organic matter, has been shown to boost our immune system, helping to suppress inflammatory diseases and improve mood. Anything that connects with the outdoors and animals gets us exposed to microorganisms that will be healers. Some of us will have to put aside the sanitary world we are culturing and get our hands in the soil, our bare feet wet on the grass and touch, sniff and feel the plants.

I can recall at least two recent instances where a guest has received great benefit from lying on the earth—one guest in summer enjoyed the textures and experience of lying in our wild grasses, taking photos up into the sky. Another guest, on a winter quiet garden day, lay in our labyrinth, spending an hour quietly noticing and enjoying the massaging nature of the pine cones on her back:

Semi-supine on a soft bed
Enfolded in a cosy coat to gaze upwards,
or inwards with eyes closed.

Bathed in scent of pine
Serenaded by sound of birdsong
Entranced by tracery of twigs above

Sensitivity heightened in repose
Perceive gentle massage with each breath
Blissfully relaxing

Forest bathing in the scents, sights, sounds
and touch of nature
Dwelling in the sacrament of non-doing.[9]

Jesus, embodying Wisdom, prayed and healed primarily in nature, often using symbols from the natural world to illustrate Wisdom. The stories he shared showed the necessity of being transformed from the inside out. He talked about how we can explore the "kingdom of heaven", which is another term for the creative insight we receive through Wisdom:

> The kingdom of heaven is like a mustard seed that someone took and sowed in his field; it is the smallest of all the seeds, but when it has grown it is the greatest of shrubs and becomes a tree, so that the birds of the air come and make nests in its branches.[10]

Finding symbols in the natural world brings in our imagination to highlight our inner issues and nurture creative insight. As we start small with our noticings in nature, and open to this insight, we find an energy that helps our insight to grow and expand; perhaps leading to a connection to other aspects of creation.

Choosing the Tree of Life

As mentioned earlier in this chapter, the symbol of the tree can speak to us of so many areas: her rootedness, ability to withstand different weathers, her connection to the earth and the sky, and the way she flourishes and waits through the seasons. Trees have exceptional senses as they can sense every chemical gradient and electromagnetic fluctuation, as well as the oxygen levels and pollution in the air.[11] They detect what is going on in the soil through their roots and complex fungi connect them to other trees, allowing them to mother their young and develop community. So it is no surprise that a great symbol of Wisdom is the Tree of Life, mentioned many times in the Bible and other sacred documents, and valued so highly as to have a place in the Holy of Holies, the sacred inner sanctuary of the Jewish Temple. The Hebrew word for tree is *etz*, which is very similar to the Hebrew word *etza*, which means wise-counsel, advice or Wisdom and thus the Jewish Torah is also referred to as The Tree of Life.[12]

The first Psalm describes the delight of opening to Wisdom and likens this to a tree that flourishes all year round. In the last chapter of the Bible, the Tree of Life is watered by the River of Life, and her leaves are for the healing of the nations.[13] Harmony and healing are Wisdom's essence. In this pictorial language the different fruits and continual fruiting of the Tree of Life highlight this new way of knowing and enlightenment that Wisdom brings forth.

An important aspect of the Tree of Life was its oil. The Old Testament priests would use myrrh, as a symbol of the oil of the Tree of Life, for anointing the eyes, indicative of finding insight into the knowledge of creation. This was a fragrant tree whose perfume would connect emotions and memory, bringing together mind and deep body-knowing.[14]

The two trees that Adam and Eve are offered in the myth at the beginning of the Bible are the Tree of Life and the Tree of the Knowledge of Good and Evil.[15] The couple are encouraged to eat the fruits of all the trees in the Garden of Eden, except from the Tree of the Knowledge of Good and Evil which represented partial knowledge with the potential for good or evil. This tree was not connected to the full unitive knowledge of embodied Wisdom. The priests and the prophets of the Old Testament believed that the knowledge of creation, the science of that time, could not be separated from Wisdom's way of binding all things together. In choosing the Tree of the Knowledge of Good and Evil, Adam and Eve were missing out on opening to the holding in harmony and the spiritual insight that the Tree of Life offered, hence allowing for a knowledge that could lead to acquiring power over creation, rather than working with creation:

> Blessed are those who find wisdom,
> those who gain understanding,
> for she is more profitable than silver
> and yields better returns than gold.
> She is more precious than rubies;
> nothing you desire can compare with her.
> She is a tree of life to those who take hold of her;
> those who hold her fast will be blessed.[16]

The earth as mother

The way of Wisdom with a deeper connection to the earth has been noted from early humans. From Neolithic times the myths, philosophies and theologies developed through noting the many aspects of nature such as life and death, the cycles of the moon and rhythms of the seasons. Ancient people revered the moon, the Virgin-Mother-Goddess—bringing the feminine image, with her power radiating out for the planting and harvesting of crops, the cycle of seasons of the earth, the ebb and flow of the tides, and the connection to the seasons of the woman's menstrual cycles.

The image of the earth was also revered and referred to as Mother Goddess, highlighting the creative spirit of Sophia, Holy Wisdom, who is like the first mother bringing forth life. There is a maternal, nurturing aspect to the earth, that connects to the sacred. Julian of Norwich in her visions reflected on Wisdom as our Mother, Wisdom being part of the Trinity that she voiced as "Strength, Wisdom and Love":

The deep wisdom of the Trinity is our Mother. In her we are all enclosed.[17]

Hildegard of Bingen speaks of the earth as mother and of the energy of the soil, speaking of its fertile ways of bringing forth life and embodying the holy:

> The earth is at the same time mother,
> she is mother of all that is natural,
> mother of all that is human.
> She is the mother of all,
> for contained in her are the seeds of all.
> The earth of humankind contains all moisture,
> all verdancy, all germinating power.
> It is in so many ways fruitful.
> All creation comes from it.
> Yet it forms not only the basic raw materials
> for humankind, but also
> the substance of Incarnation.[18]

The aspect of mothering and nurturing also encompasses the womb-like nature of this holding. Myths of creation, with the fertility of seeds planted in the darkness and being brought forth into the light, pictured the earth as a womb, giving birth to the fruit of the planted seed. In the Native Middle Eastern tradition, the womb-reality is present at the beginning. In Genesis 1, the darkness on the face of the deep is the womb that is awakened by the *ruach*, the breath, bringing inspiration and creative possibilities. Our belonging is with all the earth within this womb-like nurturing, this "big belonging".

On a nature-writing course I attended we discussed this thought-provoking concept of being inside "a big belonging". We are held inside a galaxy, therefore when we go outside of our buildings we are "inside" and when we go back into our buildings we are "outside". The buildings we spend our lives in are the alien environment where we are disconnected from the big belonging. I might be in the garden in the depths of winter, looking into the starlit sky and note a sense of being encompassed in this wider universe, within the cosmos.

The word "compassion" comes from the word for "womb" in both Hebrew and Arabic and with our increase in eco-anxiety, in what is happening to our planet, we need to find the compassion that holds and grounds us. During the anxiety of the coronavirus (Covid-19) pandemic, I explored a poem about the different ways we can find a sense of holding:

I am Held

within my body
bone and muscle shoring up my frame

within this house
with prayers oozing from each wall

within this garden
blue-tit squeak, daffodil dance, rooted tree
reminding me of my belonging
and the energy flowing
from earth to sky

in community
in the embrace of a wider weaving

within the silence
and the "thinking of you" grace of others

around the table
with the deep wisdom of my saints

with the wider energy
of my own imagination
my pink fiery dragon
taking me to reflective spaces

And the world is held
within this deep love connection
stretching around us
as the flesh of the womb
All of us, animal, plant, galaxy
held by Love
that guides us through to our emerging[19]

There is a lovely illustration of being held that happened on one of our garden days. The sun was shining and one of our guests decided to sit in the centre of our large lawn. He noticed a pigeon on the telephone wire and decided to stay still for as long as the pigeon stayed on the wire, not expecting this to last very long. However, the two of them sat for 40 minutes before the pigeon flew away. There was a real dynamic going on between the observer and observed—each being held in silent stillness. For the guest, this was a transformational time, and I wonder what happened for the pigeon. Every time this story is told, people react with amazement and reflective interest.

Our community at Holy Rood House also acts as a container, a holder, of the conflicting emotions that we experience around our commitment in climate suffering. We acknowledge our own responsibility of not caring for the world as we could, with a sense of repentance. Our training with our guests in trauma helps us to make connections with the trauma of the earth. Both areas require listening and giving whole attention to the story. Sometimes acknowledging what is, and how we feel, can help us accept this sense of lostness, our helplessness. If this is held within community, we can encourage each other to reorientate; to open ourselves to connect to the earth in a way that is right for each of us.

Spirit at the heart of everything

My father used to take our family on many beautiful walks in the Yorkshire Dales. He worked as an accountant in a firm that worked in quarries and knew about many types of stone. He often talked about "alive stones", and I would tease him about this, until I understood what he meant. He had opened himself to what stones were communicating to him, a sense of living presence. I stitched him a "living stone" piece for his eightieth birthday—and knew that the lichen, and all surrounding that stone in the scene would understand that sense of presence.

My nature explorations, through experimental creative ways, of walks in the dark, sitting by the river in all different lights and getting to know certain trees more intimately, have connected to deep desires within me, and I try and acknowledge the healing I am receiving. There is an "essence" that I detect through the rocks, trees and wildlife: an essence of the holy and a connection to my wild self.

Einstein showed that matter itself was a form of energy in his special theory of relativity. Science reveals that everything is both matter and energy. As mentioned in Chapter 2, we all have an energetic essence, as does all of creation. Wisdom is energy that shapes and holds the universe together.

Also in that chapter we explored our unique voice through the hum, finding our own resonance within us. One guest felt her hum connect to the cosmos, to something way beyond, to the "spheres". In the depth of her, a true connection to the planet. Wisdom is vibrational energy that was there at the start of the world. To tune in to this energy, we open from our deeper resonance, often coming from our heart space. We can become more attuned to both our own vibrational energy and that of creation as we walk, garden, sit and be in creation.

An aspect of this vibrational energy is felt as "song", a song of the earth. The ancient routes of the Aborigines are known as songlines. They know the land by its song. If they are finding a place in the car, their song speeds up or slows down with the speed of the car. Researchers don't know what came first: the route or the song.[20]

Finding the songs of the earth can open our listening to this vibrational energy; the sounds of wind, of water, of wildlife, can help us open to this energy. I have been out in the dawn chorus in the garden at Holy Rood House with the large array of birds, all competing with song. In May, the song from 4 a.m. is amazing: the vast repertoire of the blackbird and thrush, the lyrical tinklings of the goldfinches, the tiny wren blasting out its trills and the greenfinch "tzee" sounding two notes together. In this early sacred time, I have experienced this sense of song over me, feeling myself grow into the garden and becoming part of the earth in this transformed environment.

A guest at Holy Rood House wrote the following poem illustrating our connection of our own unique vibration with this greater vibrational energy:

Identity

Who am I?
I'm a song in the making that has never been heard before.
At any moment I am a particular note,
Heard and understood in relation to what has come before,
Shaped by the silences, and interpreted by future reiteration;
The same but different.
At times the songs of those around mean I cannot be heard
Through the mighty thunder of harmony and dissonance.
There are times when my melody merges with those around
In stately or sprightly counterpoint.
And at the end of my song it will become part of the great song of life,
Of all that was, is and will be,
Still recognizably myself but also part of the great dance,
Weaving in and out,
An essential part of the whole.[21]

We may find we connect to a sacredness as we discover our connection to the natural world, our inner "I am" connecting to a greater "I am". Saint Francis of Assisi opens us to these thoughts. He knew that divine revelation emerges from the natural world, stating this as the first book of Scripture. We are a microcosm of the whole of the cosmos—the macrocosm. What is within us we find mimicked in the natural world. The way of Wisdom helps us to open to the energy and vision of these revealings.

The integral worldview of reality where spirit is at the heart of everything, with all creation being potential revealers of this creative spirit, has evolved from a number of streams of thought from theologians, physicians, philosophers and many Native American religions. People such as Buddhist Thich Nhat Hanh, Joanna Macy, Matthew Fox and Thomas Berry for instance, all affirm spirit at the core of every created being and most essentially that this inner spirit is connected to an outer presence. Everything has an inner and outer aspect, like a spiral.[22]

In the Gospel of Thomas, Logion 3 is about finding a balance between our inner microcosm and the outer macrocosm:

> Jesus said: . . . the kingdom is within you, and it is outside of you.
> When you know yourselves, then you will be known.

The kingdom is about this different way of seeing, of finding Perspective 4—a unity within ourselves and outside of ourselves. At Holy Rood House we use the word "kin-dom", as this expresses the relational aspect of ourselves within creation through the energy life-force of Holy Wisdom. Through our connection of inner and outer we find relational aspects of the natural world that add to our belonging and holding.

We have a labyrinth in the Holy Rood House gardens—brick built by young volunteers—under the pine trees. This ancient symbol combines the imagery of the circle and the spiral, and represents the universe and creation. Walking this path, the outer leading to the inner and out again, helps us to reflect on our own connection with our inner and outer world. On my first experience of walking a labyrinth, feeling the earth beneath my feet, I got to one particular spot that just resonated with where I was in life. I was very aware of the tension of what I could see and feel as the outer world around me and the centre of the labyrinth that I was moving towards. I stayed at this mid-point, listening for what the labyrinth was telling me at that time.

Teilhard de Chardin, a Jesuit priest, devoted his life to researching this relational aspect, bringing religion and science, spirit and matter, together. He was concerned that the universe had lost its centre, which for him was Christ, this life-energy also known as Wisdom. This energy and unity of Wisdom he could see in the entire cosmos, from the smallest fragment to relationships in community. He believed that personal divine love is invested organically with all of creation, unifying the world:

Driven by the forces of love, the fragments of the world seek each other so that the world may come to being. In the divine milieu, all the elements of the universe touch each other by that which is most inward and ultimate in them.[23]

Caring for the earth

We need to find the communities that help us to care for the earth together, connected to our passions. I accompanied a person in her early twenties, who was living with ME or Chronic Fatigue. She remembered that at the age of eight, after the death of her grandfather, she had a realization that we all die. Throughout her teens, she often suffered from depression and had increasing anxiety over the state of the earth and our survival on this planet. The question that was around for her was "What is the point if we are all going to die?". When we started to work together, she could only walk a few steps as her energy was so poor. We worked together for a couple of years, over which time we especially looked at her gifts and passions. We looked at what she wanted her life shaped by. She tapped into a knowing within her and came to one session excited as she *knew* the point to her life that was connected to love, through her loved ones, especially her grandfather. Her energy improved as she realized that her concern over climate change and our survival on the earth was something that she was passionate about, and that she could link into groups where she could contribute. Life became something vital to her, and she found ways of linking to the earth with walking and cycling and sharing this experience with others.

This illustrates how important it is to honour our own uniqueness and what we hear from the earth. How we care for the earth is influenced through our own noticings and listenings to ourselves and the earth. Within each of us is the message of the universe, one we can listen to and voice as we engage with creation and her transformative ways:

We cannot live securely in a world which is not our own, in a world which is interpreted for us by others. An interpreted world is not a home. Part of the terror is to take back our own listening,

to put our ears to our own inner voices, to see our own light,
which is our birthright, and comes to us in silence.[24]

As we come to the end of this chapter, whatever our thoughts on the
different aspects presented, we note our calling for awareness of our
interdependence with all forms of life, and to explore their worth and
way of Wisdom. Our community has regular ecology meetings to discuss
our place and belonging with all of creation. The word "ecology" is a
derivation from the Greek word *oikos* meaning "home", and included
in our meetings is how we encourage relationship with the earth and
re-member our rightful place in creation, within our environment of
hospitality and healing. We are assisted by responding to the abundance
and essential blessing of creation which draws us to wonderment and
thanksgiving, helping to inspire and sustain our work for justice and
peace:

> Once we have "fallen in love outwards", once we have experienced
> the fierce joy of life that attends extending our identity into nature,
> once we realize that the nature within and the nature without are
> continuous, then we too may share and manifest the exquisite
> beauty and effortless grace associated with the natural world.[25]

Creative ideas for connecting to Wisdom of the earth

An interesting exercise for exploring our connection with the earth is
to reflect on our eco-story. This is our story of our memories of the
natural world and how we connect in the present. It doesn't have to
be complicated—maybe a mind map with "eco-story" written in the
middle and then seeing what words or images emerge. This can help us
understand any reluctance to venture out, as well as how we would like to
explore. We may want to replicate what we enjoyed as children. Keeping
in touch with our eco-story can help us to articulate something of what
happens to us when we experience the natural world. The intimate
experiences we can have might be hard to express in words and there may
be a way of marking these occasions with collected objects or in image.

Wherever we live there is always the natural world, with its creative energy pushing through. Plants appearing through cracks in the concrete and the sound of the wind in telegraph wires give us opportunity for connection. We need to find times of play, exploration and listening as we venture outdoors. Connecting to our breath in the natural elements can feel different from when we are indoors. Letting our body lead, using our senses, can take us on adventures in the natural environment and to explore what we notice.

We can use the natural world for experimenting, whether it is with foraging, photography or flying a kite. As a creative pursuit, I took some pieces of material and buried them in different places in the garden. I wanted to see what the earth and compost would mark on these light-coloured materials. The white material that came out of the compost was the most exciting—once rinsed, spots of pink, blue and yellow colours had been dyed into the cloth. Other pieces revealed interesting shapes that I made into stitched pieces. It was a way for me to connect emotionally and physically to the earth around me.

Our own wild nature is often suppressed and going out in different seasons and elements, experiencing the dark, the cold, the heat and the rain, can awaken our own wildness, rooted deep within. Finding the vibrations and sounds that resonate can connect to our deeper subtle energies.

Exploring our environment through differing emotions will mean that we notice other aspects of creation. The natural world has ways of highlighting how to be with chaos, darkness, death and decay. At our most difficult moments, nature can often break through. I know when I experienced an especially challenging day there appeared a double rainbow, and at another time butterflies alighting on a hand after a funeral. One of our guests, in her deep grief, was able to explore with watching the buddleia in her garden change from blooming to decay. She spent time conversing with and painting this buddleia, finding out what it needed to share with her.

We can keep a connection from our inner core to the outer core by finding ways that keep that thread. We might have times of having the curtains open at night to experience sleeping with night-sky connection, for instance. There are some sturdy pine trees at the end of our garden that I can see from the window in the flat. I often use these trees in my reflecting. They are outside in the "inside", holding a presence within myself. They anchor me to the presence of something more. They take me to the wider perspective, so I don't get caught in my internal loop and chatter.

Another way of exploring inner and outer is through the labyrinth. There are many in the UK and around the world. If you are unable to find one near you, there are finger labyrinths online which provide a mindful way of exploring.[26]

Wisdom

Wisdom you are the centre of the Universe
The motion of the Earth
You are in the rising of the sun
The going down of the moon
In the movement of the sea

Your justice spans the World
Strong, silent yet fluid
Reaching out to all in need
You are at the Centre of our being
Feeding and nurturing
The word made flesh

Standing at the crossroads
Strengthening, Guiding, Encouraging
Yet Soft and Yielding
Father, Mother, Lover and Friend.[27]

Notes

1   <https://www.bbc.co.uk/news/health-43674270>.

2   These perspectives have incorporated my own lived experience and have included ideas from Serge King, "Seeing is Believing: The Four Worlds of a Shaman", in Gary Doore, *Shaman's Path: Healing, Personal Growth and Empowerment* (Boston, MA: Shambhala, 1988), pp. 48–52.

3   From an expanded translation of Proverbs 1:7; Neil Douglas-Klotz, *Desert Wisdom: A Nomad's Guide to Life's Big Questions from the Heart of the Native Middle East* (Worthington: ARC Books, 2011), p. 94.

4   Joanna Macy, quoted in Alex Wildwood, *A Faith to Call my Own* (London: Quaker Home Service, 1999), p. 39.

5   Jerry Spinelli, *Stargirl* (New York: Orchard Books, 2000), <https://www.goodreads.com/work/quotes/963221-stargirl>.

6   Thornborough Henges, near Masham, North Yorkshire, DL8 2RA.

7   *Rilke's Book of Hours: Love Poems to God*, trs and eds Anita Barrows and Joanna Macy (New York: Riverhead Books, 1997), II, 16.

8   Rachel Corbett, *You Must Change Your Life: The Story of Rainer Maria Rilke and Auguste Rodin* (New York: W. W. Norton & Company, 2016), <https://www.poetryfoundation.org/poetrymagazine/articles/90278/from-you-must-change-your-life-the-story-of-rainer-maria-rilke-and-auguste-rodin>.

9   Helen Leathard.

10 Matthew 13:31–2.

11 Information from Stefano Mancuso, in his book *Brilliant Green*; Miguel Mindonca, *Wisdom: Now and Always* (independently published, 2020).

12 <https://blogs.timesofisrael.com/tree-tips/>; <https://www.hebrewversity.com/advice-life-hebrew-meaning-biblical-tree-life/>.

13 Revelation 22:1,2 and 14. Margaret Barker, *Wisdom and the Stewardship of Knowledge*, <http://www.margaretbarker.com/Papers/WisdomAndThe StewardshipOfKnowledge.pdf>.

14 Wisdom is also described as the oil itself in the book of Sirach (Ecclesiasticus) 24:15.

15 Genesis 2:9.

16 Proverbs 3:13–15,18 (NIV).

[17] Mother Julian of Norwich, *Revelations of Divine Love*, trs and eds Halcyon Backhouse and Rhona Pipe (London: Hodder & Stoughton, 1987), fourteenth revelation, Chapter 54, p. 113.

[18] Hildegard of Bingen, <https://friendsofsilence.net/quote/2008/04/earth-same-time-mother-she-mother-all-natural>.

[19] Author's poem, March 2020 in lockdown due to coronavirus. Previously unpublished.

[20] Bruce Chatwin BBC programme. Bruce Chatwin, *The Songlines: Bruce Chatwin* (Vintage Books, 1998).

[21] Guest at Holy Rood House, *Poetry and Art from Holy Rood House: A Celebration of 25 Years 1993–2018* (independently published, 2019), p. 1 73.

[22] Walter Wink, *The Powers that Be* (New York: Doubleday, 1989), Chapter 1.

[23] <https://www.brainyquote.com/quotes/pierre_teilhard_de_chardi_389379>.

[24] Elaine Bellezza, "Hildegard of Bingen, Warrior of Light", *Gnosis* 21 (1991), *Gnosis* magazine.

[25] John Seed, quoted in Alistair McIntosh, *Soil and Soul: People versus Corporate Power* (London: Aurum Press, an imprint of Quarto Publishing, 2004), p. 118.

[26] <https://labyrinthsinbritain.uk/map-of-uk-labyrinths-mazes/>, to find nearest labyrinth in the UK. Finger labyrinth—google images.

[27] Guest at Holy Rood House, *Poetry and Art from Holy Rood House: A Celebration of 25 Years 1993–2018*, p. 26.

CHAPTER 6

Wisdom as a way of transformation

This pilgrimage has begun
Journey deep within you to the place you can now call home.[1]

Throughout this book, we have explored the vast range of treasures that Wisdom offers. Wisdom as process, as an enlightening, opens up a way of transforming as we go through our lives. The following are some highlights of the many aspects of Wisdom's process that we have so far explored:

- Beginning with the body we open to our spaciousness within; using our breath and senses we find a deeper resonance where we open to our own truth.
- It is through the present moment that a way of Wisdom opens to the next step, for a knowing to emerge.
- The creative process of opening to our deep body-knowing helps us to explore healing ways, leading us through darkness, finding a deeper energy and a calmer centre.
- Through opening to this deep knowing we find our true image: who we are without all our roles and baggage and who we are in the sexual skin that is a comfortable fit.
- Wisdom is relational and opens a way for a relation with our own self, as well as to all other creatures and the earth, through a unifying with divine Love.
- The way of Wisdom leads us into community—within ourselves and to others. She opens the way of compassion, a way connected to love, that helps us find our voice for justice and peace.

- Through the way of Wisdom, we open to a sense of belonging, at home within ourselves and more unified within our environment.
- Opening to the way of Wisdom helps us explore our song that unites with the song of the earth.

In this concluding chapter, we consider how we can live a life open to the process of Wisdom, what is needed for this open awareness, and how this can become a way of life, leading to a way of peace-making, healing and unity with creation.

I am hopeful that this book has already provided the impetus for each of us to carve out space to open Wisdom's way. Our lives can so easily feel cluttered, and we may need some reflection on the spaces we require for more exploring. Anything that involves change in our lives can be perceived as a threat to the order we try and create. We may have to challenge what might be stopping us from opening to our senses and a deeper presence:

> The spiritual journey from beginning to end can be characterized
> as the overcoming of fear.[2]

We may need to consider our habits, our way of thought, our beliefs and our disciplines (or lack of disciplines). We can consider what does clutter our energy and thoughts—what is our input during the day that might add to worry, stress, and busyness? Perhaps the political news, social media and lack of relaxation might come into these considerations.

It is important to note that the way of Wisdom is also the way of wellbeing; a way of calming, reducing stress, of better mental, physical, emotional and spiritual health. Suggestions for treatment for Long-Covid, for instance, include stimulation of the vagal nerves, which carry signals between our brain, heart and digestive system and are a key part of our parasympathetic nervous system. Activities that open to our deep body-knowing such as deeper breathing exercises, humming, chanting, yoga and foot massage all stimulate the vagal nerves, taking us away from the stress response and calming our nervous system.

As we drop down to a deeper resonance within, our heart space, we connect to the electromagnetic field generated by the heart which is

60 times greater in amplitude than the field of brainwaves. These are measurable several feet outside of the body and scientists have found that breathing exercises where we open to this heart space help the electromagnetic field of the heart sync with the electromagnetic field of the brain.³ Most of us feel out of kilter as our brain and heart are not running in a unified way. The disciplines to open to Wisdom, such as contemplative practices or ways of coming into stillness, help us feel more coherent and radiant. Though the way of Wisdom may challenge, the rewards include peace, joy, and enlightenment. As we link to her ways, we will find we want more, we will want to prioritize ways of deeper connection, caught up in the exciting journey exploring our uniqueness and our connection to the earth.

Esther de Waal in her book exploring the inner and outer worlds talks about having hopeful expectations of a more worthwhile life:

> Am I willing to cross the threshold of new understanding by being open and receptive, not closed in and defensive? ... The most profound threshold, however, remains that between the inner and outer, between going deeper into the interior self and emerging to meet the world beyond the self without protective defences, as friend not foe.⁴

Opening ourselves to this way of being requires a vulnerability, a letting go of our need to control and of defences that may be stopping us connecting to this deeper way. We can be expectant to new ways, to finding a new song within us that resonates with the unity of creation. Listening is a key skill to finding this new way: listening to our deep body-knowing, to inspiring stories, to wise people and the Wisdom of the earth.

The way of Wisdom starts with the small, the noticing of the little things in life that lift our energy and connect to our passions. We learn to cherish our revelations and to appreciate beauty, words of love spoken, textures, shapes and colours that give us joy. The Quaker Isaac Penington spoke of the importance of noticing the small, before we are able to grasp the meaning of the greater philosophies of life. He also reiterates how our journey of exploration starts in the darkness, in uncertainty, with more light or enlightenment as we explore:

> Thou must join in with the beginnings of life, and be exercised
> with the day of small things, before thou meet with the great
> things, wherein is the clearness and satisfaction of the soul. The
> rest is at noonday; but the travels begin at the breakings of day,
> wherein are but glimmerings or little light, wherein the discovery
> of good and evil are not so manifest and certain; yet there must
> the traveller begin and travel; and in his faithful travels . . . the
> light will break in upon him more and more.[5]

The way of Wisdom in our earlier trials will feel like we are groping around in the dark. Discernment is a gift we can cultivate, on our own or with accompaniment, to feel our way through what works for us and what is not working. It is in this darkness, through the testing of different disciplines and ways of searching, that we find what resonates, what gives us those "Ah ha" moments. We find the truth in what resonates with us, so our own truth may differ from others' truth, although all truths will connect us to oneness and unity. We may need to have many trials to find a way to this truth. The stories in the Bible of both Jacob and Job have them questing and wrestling to find the truth that helps them through their suffering as well as uniting them with who they truly are. Through their questioning and tussles they find answers that settle and show a way of union and relationship with the Knower.[6]

Through this questing our lives can become more purposeful and we cultivate a curiosity that leads us to further searching. As we explore our own truth that resonates with our depth, we find that this truth resonates out, or echoes in other places and circumstances. We follow the threads of our curiosity and are led on a journey of exploration. Our lives are broadened from working out the everyday through mainly problem-solving, to a wider field with creative inspiration where we find a resonance of what is inside us with what is outside of us:

> For what is inside of you is what is outside of you,
> and the one who fashions you on the outside
> is the one who shaped the inside of you.
> And what you see outside of you, you see inside of you;
> it is visible and it is your garment.[7]

As we cultivate how to listen to our inner being we find what gestates within. These are the seeds of our purpose and desires. Our disciplines can help create the right environment for the flow of Wisdom, the flow of right energy to allow our seeds to respond and grow.

This new way of knowing, our intuitive knowledge, springs forth from the present moment. These are *kairos* moments, *kairos* meaning "deep time", or "qualitative time". *Chronos* is the time we live by and run our lives, and *kairos* moments are the new insights that come as a flash of inspiration. Both words come from the Ancient Greek with Kairos being the Greek god of opportunity, a god of winged feet that darted about and could only be caught by one who was alert.

The immediate knowledge of the *kairos* moment Eckhart calls the "spark of the soul"[8] which links what is created in us to what is uncreated, and the *kairos* moment to the eternal now—an experience of all reality in the present moment. We form a relationship between the created and uncreated, between the known and the Knower behind all knowing. It is a relationship of love.

Disciplines for this way include finding a rhythm that suits our individuality. Appendix 2 will explore some ideas. I started my exploring through journaling and other creative ways of exploring the long-term suffering I was going through. This led to ways of understanding my body and finding disciplines to keep connected to my body such as breathing exercises and yoga. These have been added to over the years, so there is always something I do daily, such as acupressure, to help with body energy and listening and reflecting to body Wisdom. I can now recognize my inner nudges that encourage an early morning walk, a creative time, a reflective space of sitting and listening, a nudge to message someone. My dreams are included in my reflections. I found contemplation helpful, and this led me to the Quakers where their discipline of coming into stillness and being held in the silence of listening is a key part of exploring my way of Wisdom. Here I experience the way of Wisdom in a community where we are all seeking inspiration and listening to the intuitive presence, all held within the great beating heart of love.

Through living and working at Holy Rood House I experience the importance of a gentle rhythm of prayer, tea breaks and mealtimes. Some guests require more structure, as they want either distraction, or assistance with how to be with their own presence when they stay with us. They can be helped with accompaniment, where they may be assisted in being with the "is-ness" of what they are going through. It is learning that it is in the non-doing times that we often open to the way of Wisdom. I had one guest who could not settle at Holy Rood; she found she just wanted to run away. The guest knew she was seeing me the next day, so managed distraction techniques to help with the anxiety, so she could get through to the next day, where she was going to come to the session and tell me she was leaving. The guest eventually managed to get to sleep and found herself waking only half-an-hour before our meeting. She awoke with a poem forming. With the long night of "staying with" something had awoken her internal healer, her deep body-knowing, and out poured this lovely poem.

Stay

Stay in this place of safety
You do not need to run
Breathe in this place of safety
Capture Divine Love
Stay in this place of safety where new life has begun
Breathe in this place of safety
Capture Divine Love

Stay in this place of safety where new life has begun
Breathe in this place of safety
Capture Divine Love
Inhale the sense of peace

Stay in this place of safety
There is no need to run
Stay
Breathe
Stay
Breathe
Stay
Breathe
Cling on to this feeling of safety
This will guide you through the storm
An anchor in the raging seas
Your compass each new dawn
Breathe in this sense of safety
There is no need to run

Stay in this place of safety where new life has begun
Breathe in this place of safety
Capture Divine Love
Inhale the presence of peace

Stay
Breathe
Stay
Breathe
Stay
Breathe
Safety is within you
There is no need to run
Stop in this place of safety
Slow down
Breathe in deeply
This pilgrimage has begun
Journey deep within you to the place you can now call home
This is your place of safety
Where your heart has a home
Stay in this place of safety
Breathe in this place of safety
Stay in this place of safety
Breathe in this place of safety
Stay
Breathe
Stay
Breathe
Stay
Breathe
Welcome Home[9]

This guest stayed, having experienced the *kairos* moment through her waiting, finding the holding of her deeper presence and finding that she could voice the Wisdom from this deeper resonance. As we experience these *kairos* moments, we can help others have the confidence to be with "what is". We can help to hold the sense of battleground within and around us, knowing that there are these breakthrough moments.

I try to observe our own community, stepping back to have a wider perspective, and it was in one of my reflections that I had an image of our guests coming with their inner labyrinth into our community, with some guests already exploring their labyrinth and others unable to connect. In this image, our community was like a gentle holding, open to, and held in, a wider space within the environment and the earth. Within the holding, we have the ability to connect to healing and health, learning and the process of transformation.

The labyrinth reflects an ancient way, one where the inner journey will feel like it winds back and forth, in and out. Communities can help us to open to our own labyrinthine journeys, to have the sense of accompaniment in our lostness. Joseph Campbell in the book *The Hero's Journey* describes how we find our self at the centre of our labyrinth, linking into the path that others help us to pursue:

> We have not even to risk the adventure alone for the heroes of all time have gone before us; the labyrinth is thoroughly known; we have only to follow the thread of the hero-path. And where we had thought to find an abomination, we shall find a God; where we had thought to slay another, we shall slay ourselves; where we had thought to travel outward, we shall come to the center of our own existence; where we had thought to be alone, we shall be with all the world.[10]

There are many fantastic examples of those who have gone before us showing us the way of Wisdom. Throughout this book, I have given a flavour of wise people who have inspired myself to a way of Wisdom such as Hildegard of Bingen, Meister Eckhart, Jesus, Mary (mother of Jesus), Julian of Norwich as well as more recent examples, including Rainer Maria Rilke, Etty Hillesum, Marsha Linehan, and many other inspirational writers. We will have our own heroes and heroines that have gone before us, and it is important to realize that as we explore, *we* become the heroes and heroines who can accompany others.

In the Gospel of Thomas, Jesus tells the disciples that when they are asked for the sign of Wisdom within, to answer with the reply "It is a movement and a rest".[11] It is finding the balance between doing and being, action and in-action, reflection and spontaneity. Finding the right rhythm, like our breathing in and breathing out, is where our energy flows naturally. Resting is just as important as the movement: with time for reflection, for being in the now, for getting into our alpha rhythms. There are many times in our lives where we experience fatigue, a lowering of energies. Pacing our lives becomes more vital at these periods, and I often mention the idea of pillars within our day. Times of stopping, of pausing to rest, to connect to our body and come into the present moment. These pauses can be revitalizing, with letting go of what is whirring around in our heads and just being with what is:

> The rhythm of the phases of action and stillness has an intelligence of its own. If we tune in, we can hear that rhythm, and the organ of perception is the desire, the nudge of excitement or the feeling of flow, of rightness, of alignment. It is a feeling of being alive. To listen to that feeling and to trust it is a profound revolution indeed.[12]

Meister Eckhart refers to finding the way of Wisdom as a search, as a quest that requires the rhythm of gentle detachment and fiery passion.[13] The observer stance of standing back from ourselves and connecting to what we notice provides this detachment of not getting caught up in our thoughts and our emotions (noted in Chapters 1 and 2). Our witness takes us to a deeper awareness where we release a flow of energy that fuels our "fiery passions" as we live with and share our deeper body-knowing. For Meister Eckhart divine knowledge can only be arrived at through the tension of the opposites, for example the rhythm of the movement and rest, the experiences between dark and light and our observations of death and life. We could consider a statement to be both true and untrue, allowing our own stretching of our limited knowledge to reach out to a deeper way of knowing. These perceived opposites are held together in Wisdom's all-embracing unity.

We are not designed to live solely in a spiritual realm or in the purely sensual realm. The way of Wisdom comes through our ordinary life with all its emotions and instabilities. We have the ability through the way of Wisdom to connect to reality *and* mystery, to grounded earthiness and what might be termed "heaven". Our spaciousness within is like a door that opens us to our own reality, as well as to the mystery of the greater beating heart that is a unitive force. This is a threshold space, where, as creators through our insights, we must stand *between the Invisible and the visible, the Unsayable and the sayable, Non-being and Being*.[14]

One of our fears when exploring a new way of being may be with this sense of openness, with connecting to our inner "door" and exploring the deeper areas. We tend to have our comfort zone behind a closed door—one where we feel safe, although possibly limited. We may find an image of an opening door, one where light beckons, a helpful one to explore. We can connect to what does entice us and draw us to new ways. There are often new ideas, of what intrigues and fascinates us, on our periphery that we can bring into our nearer vision, however wild they might seem. The way of Wisdom connects to being open-hearted *and* open-minded, perhaps thinking outside of "the box".

Another way of exploring this threshold space is through the images of a grounded part of us holding our exploring part. When I am accompanying guests in their questings, we often talk about having one foot firmly planted in the now, in the life and environment that we inhabit, in the present. This is the grounded foot, that connects our body to the earth. We then have the option of the other foot to explore the stretches of the imagination, the wild and the chaotic. The various seasons we experience, our emotional stretchings, our intellectual pursuits and the health issues we face for example, can take us to these wild wanderings. This foot can be the explorer, who experiences the mad and the unboundaried, knowing that the other foot is planted firm. Both feet help us explore our spiritual journey—the present alongside the season we explore. The way of Wisdom helps with this coordination as we find the truth and insight needed in our travels.

The way of Wisdom wakes us up to our own uniqueness, to our own calling. I had an important dream about this sense of awakening. In this dream, I am asleep and yet I have a sense of urgency, of action and purpose that wakens me and propels me out of bed. I find myself walking, below ground level, into a church that is closing down. People are carrying ancient wooden artefacts, made of golden-brown wood, with ornate carvings. A woman with a loud voice is directing the operation. I find her too loud and ask her to pipe down, as it is 2.30 a.m. and I want to go back to sleep! She wants me to get excited about these beautiful artefacts. As I move through this church, I knock over one of the artefacts and am worried it will break, but it somehow springs upright. I notice it is a carved wooden baby, cocooned in a wooden safe holding. This holding is on a big spring, so if knocked it will always right itself. My journey through this basement area leads up a tunnel where I come into the open air to a stunning view, a cliff edge where, from the safety of the green grass, I can see out to the ocean. It is awe inspiring: bright sunlight with lots of birds.

There are many aspects to this dream, beginning with the calling for my own awakening. We can be summoned in various ways: with an inner voice, a nudging that our life has to change, with a sense of lostness or of wanting more from our lives. The voice of Wisdom nudges us at the times we are at crossroads, in transition spaces, in the changes of our seasons:

> Wisdom summons you in her goodness, saying, Come to me, all of you, O foolish ones, that you may receive a gift, the understanding which is good and excellent.[15]

In this dream, a church is closing down. This could represent our old ideals that need to shift, in order to find the new way. To move from the old, we have to let go into uncharted territory, places where we have not travelled before. As mentioned in Chapter 4, it is often our sense of being lost that takes us to places with no maps. We need ways in our lives that shift us into the mystery where we find a movement, where from the nothingness Wisdom arises.

At Holy Rood House, we discover these unmapped places together— our guests help us to trust the creative energy and Wisdom that emerges from these unknown lands. We help with accompanying the traveller and encouraging the spirit of adventure, knowing that as we travel, often through darkness and pain, we learn how to get through, how to explore, often finding an uplifting and hopefulness through discovery.

This dream encompassed a sense of inner exploration, of the urgency of the Wisdom call, through a route where the baby is cocooned and not able to be knocked over. We need these nurturing images within our journeys. Wisdom's way connects us to this nurturing aspect, where the baby is never thrown out of the holding. It speaks of the womb image, of the inner gestation in the cocooned space that is birthed into the outer cosmos: the inner to outer movement of Wisdom's way. I emerged into an open space that connects to the wild, a wild expansiveness that if I acted it out I would stretch, dance and leap about. It connects to a sense of spaciousness, energy and exploring, which, if voiced, would be a singing, exuberant voice with no reputation.

There is also a director involved with the change. The director is needed to wake me up and show me the beauty of the ancient artefacts stored within the basement. We will all have this part of us, this nudger, that contains the voice of Wisdom. She will be part of the voice calling us to sort out our life, to quest for truth and a way through. We may resonate with this voice through a different character we see in a film or read in a book, through other people or inspirational texts. This is a subpersonality we can explore within ourselves.

> The breeze at dawn has secrets to tell you.
> Don't go back to sleep.

> You must ask for what you really want.
> Don't go back to sleep.

> People are going back and forth across the doorsill
> where the two worlds touch.

> The door is round and open.
> Don't go back to sleep.[16]

The coming into the light in the dream, onto this edge space, also speaks to me of being on the margins. The Wisdom way tends to evolve from the edges—from the margins of society, anywhere we feel alien. This vast, open view connects to the cosmic link of Wisdom. The way of Wisdom opens us to the immenseness of the universe. We move from our own small world to consider our unity with the whole of creation.

For Hildegard of Bingen, Wisdom is the keeper of the cosmic order. Hildegard finds divine revelation and Wisdom in all creatures of the universe. For Hildegard, the way of Wisdom only comes through struggle, challenge, pain and confusion. She recognized that Wisdom is an elusive treasure and wrote of the struggle to search out this treasure and the joy that comes from finding Wisdom:

> With Wisdom there always comes new and simple gifts and the older they become, the richer they are.[17]

In an earlier quote, Wisdom summons us to receive a gift and understanding. Wisdom gifts us *a high priestly garment which is woven from every Wisdom.*

The verse goes on to say:

> Clothe yourself with Wisdom like a robe, put knowledge upon you like a crown and be seated upon a throne of perception.[18]

Wisdom weaves and integrates, weaving a sacred garment that covers us with her healing knowing. In the ancient scriptures the high priest's woven garment included gold thread to symbolize divine Wisdom. In the original Hebrew of the Proverbs 8:23 verse where Wisdom is speaking— *Ages ago I was set up*—if one letter is changed it can read—*Ages ago I was weaving.* The image of Wisdom as weaver reiterates Wisdom's way as unifying, as holding all things together in harmony. From the beginning, she wove the web of creation:

> I, Wisdom, bind together heavenly and earthly things as a unity for the good of the people.[19]

In the oldest known complete Gospel text, the *Infancy Gospel of James*, there is a story of Mary, mother of Jesus, as a temple weaver, weaving a new veil for the temple, whilst pregnant with Jesus. The veil or temple curtain, woven of linen and including colours representing the four elements of earth, air, fire and water, was the boundary of the Holy of Holies, the symbolic space of the presence of God. Mary is revered as the bearer of Wisdom, starting with her openness to say "Yes" to giving birth to what waits within. She seeks community with her cousin Elizabeth to assist with the tensions of waiting in her pregnancy. The birth of Jesus through the nativity reflects the door opening to bring forth what Mary had conceived within. Various visitors to this nativity gave messages that Mary reflected upon, through her pondering heart, reiterating her way of staying open to her Wisdom.[20]

The woven robe that symbolizes Wisdom's gift is a wonderful psychological image. This is like an invisible protective cloak around us that may enable courage and confidence. I often introduce this image with people I accompany, especially if they are feeling vulnerable and finding it difficult to face the challenges of life. We can imagine we are clothed in this nurturing garment that helps integrate and harmonize us within our communities and environments.

The image of Wisdom as a robe connects to what Hildegard saw as an inner "tent". Her image of the tent is that it comes folded up in us at our birth, as original blessings. To obtain Wisdom one must search out these blessings and recover our original Wisdom. Hildegard encourages us to find strength in being constant, in being compassionate and self-critical regarding our motivations. She suffered extreme illness throughout her life and found that these times of immobility would only lift if she listened to the nudges of Wisdom's way, and made herself follow her calling. The work of creativity was part of this process as Hildegard could vouch for the birth of Wisdom through all her creative explorings of visions, music compositions, poetry and writing.

Hildegard spoke of our priority as unfurling of the divine presence within ourselves. She saw how community can be formed when we all join to unfurl the divine tent that exists in all creation birthing a living community that is compassionate, hope-filled and wise.

The tent image is found in the Wisdom tradition representing the divine presence of *shekinah* (which has various spellings). *Shekinah* comes from the Hebrew word meaning "dwelling" or "settling" and denotes the presence of God in a nurturing way, connecting to the divine feminine. In Jewish mysticism, *shekinah* was associated with the clouds of glory, which guided the Israelites during their wandering in the desert, and the pillar of fire that warmed them at night—a protective maternal presence in the bewildering journey of the Israelites.[21]

There is a beautiful allegory in the Wisdom book of Sirach, where Wisdom speaks of her story:

> I came forth from the mouth of the Most High
> and covered the earth like a mist.

and how she traversed over all the earth and over all people and nations. She speaks of her yearning for a resting place and how the

> Creator of all things gave me a command,
> and my Creator chose the place for my tent.

This tent was where Wisdom could minister.

> I took root in an honoured people

And from this root she blossoms:

> Like the vine I bud forth delights,
> and my blossoms become glorious and abundant fruit.

Through this beautiful speech, Wisdom speaks of her way, the flow of her movement from inward to an outward vastness:

> I was like a canal from a river,
> like a water channel into a garden.
> I said, "I will water my garden
> and drench my flower-beds."
> And lo, my canal became a river,
> and my river a sea.

And finally we note her purpose through this movement:

> I will again make instruction shine forth like the dawn,
> and I will make it clear from far away.
> I will again pour out teaching like prophecy,
> and leave it to all future generations.
> Observe that I have not laboured for myself alone,
> but for all who seek wisdom.[22]

So it is from the vastness of Wisdom's influence that she finds her dwelling within people, and from this root she blossoms and opens out to flow back into the vastness. Her way allows our own connection to our deepest centre to flow out to this vast sea of eternity.

This dwelling within, that connects us to divine presence, also gives us an understanding of home. Finding this dwelling helps us to locate a sense of belonging, a space where we understand our reflections and come home to our true selves. My questing with Wisdom has taught me how to be: to be with myself, to be with what is going on around me and feel at home with myself. I like my own space, my own being and feel at home in my own skin. I never feel alone, as I have a sense of accompaniment through Wisdom. She gives me a confidence that all will be well. Having solitary time is important for me to keep in touch with listening and reflecting on her call. This calling is empowering, providing momentum and highlighting my vocation alongside my responsibilities. The image I have is of climbing a mountain where Wisdom's call draws me onwards and upwards. I need to climb, and although this is hard, I find an energy flow from my breath, my body and from the earth. I discover the tools I need as I journey. There is shelter, spaces for stopping and to admire the views. I climb with a knowing that this is what I have to do, and will always do.

As we find our truth and connect to a wider perspective that challenges us to cosmic justice, we might find a way to speak out. If we speak out from what Wisdom reveals, we may find that we awaken others. Logion 88 in the Gospel of Thomas is about the prophet coming to awaken within us what already belongs to us. As we find our Wisdom voice, we become the prophet and give to others what already belongs to them, what they know deep down. This book is my calling from Wisdom, and it is my hope that Wisdom will call to the reader's deep knowing, to awaken and lead others to find their calling from Wisdom. This is the way of community and unity for all creation.

> Once upon a time there was Wisdom. There was Wisdom, and she was present everywhere with all the intensity and all the desire of all there was. And once the Word was spoken she alone dived into the spaces between the words, blessing the silence out

of which new worlds are born. Now as it was in the beginning,
Wisdom is hearing all creation into speech. She alone knows
something of the possibilities.[23]

The beautiful dance of Wisdom, the flow of love in and around us, is a
fitting end to this book. Hildegard captures this dance through her vision
of Wisdom having three wings. One wing explores mystery, one wing
explores reality, and the third flows between the two to keep balance and
the tune for the song that enfolds the world. The following composition
O virtus Sapientiae translates as:

> O the power of Wisdom:
> You, in circling, encircle all things,
> You are embracing everything in a way that brings life into being.
> Three wings you have:
> one soars above into the heights,
> one from the earth exudes,
> and all about now flies the third.
> Praise be to you, as is your due, O Wisdom.[24]

Notes

[1]   Lynn McEwan, "Stay" —used with permission. Previously unpublished.

[2]   Kabir Edmund Helminski, *Living Presence (Revised): The Sufi Path to Mindfulness and the Essential Self* (New York: Tarcher Perigee, 2017), Chapter 22.

[3]   <https://www.heartmath.org/>.

[4]   Esther de Waal, *Living on the Border* (Norwich: Canterbury Press, 2011), p. 3.

[5]   *Quaker Faith and Practice*, fifth edition (Oxford: Berforts Information Press, 2013), 19:43.

[6]   Jacob wrestling is found in Genesis 32. Job's questing goes through most of the book of Job.

[7]   *The Thunder, Perfect Mind*, from the Nag Hammadi Library, tr. George W. MacRae.

8   Matthew Fox, *Meister Eckhart: A Mystic Warrior for our Times* (Novato, CA: New World Library, 2014), p. 189.

9   Lynn McEwan, "Stay"—used with permission. Previously unpublished.

10 Quoted in On-Being podcast with Richard Rohr.

11 Gospel of Thomas, Logion 50.

12 Charles Eisenstein, *The More Beautiful World Our Hearts Know Is Possible* (Berkeley, CA: North Atlantic Books, 2013), <https://www.goodreads. com/work/quotes/24084470-the-more-beautiful-world-our-hearts-know- is-possible?page=2>.

13 Cyprian Smith, *The Way of Paradox: Spiritual Life as Taught by Meister Eckhart* (London: Darton, Longman & Todd, 1987), p. 26.

14 *A Year with Rilke: Daily Readings from the Best of Rainer Maria Rilke*, trs and eds Anita Barrows and Joanna Macy (New York: HarperCollins, 2009), introduction.

15 From *The Teaching of Silvanus* 41 (one of the texts found at Nag Hamadi in 1945).

16 Coleman Barks, *Essential Rumi* (San Francisco: Harper San Francisco, 1995), p. 35.

17 *Hildegard of Bingen's Scivias: Know the Ways*, tr. Bruce Hozeski (Sante Fe, CA: Bear & Company, 1986). Quote of Hildegard from the introduction by Matthew Fox.

18 *The Teaching of Silvanus* 41.

19 *Hildegard of Bingen's Scivias: Know the Ways*, tr. Bruce Hozeski (Sante Fe, CA: Bear & Company, 1986). Quote of Hildegard from the introduction by Matthew Fox.

20 Luke 2:19.

21 <https://www.myjewishlearning.com/article/ the-divine-feminine-in-kabbalah-an-example-of-jewish-renewal/>.

22 Sirach (or Ecclesiasticus) 24:3,8,12,17,30–4.

23 Lucy Tatman, in June Boyce-Tillman, *Unconventional Wisdom (Gender, Theology and Spirituality)* (London: Equinox, 2007), p. 40.

24 June Boyce-Tillman, *Unconventional Wisdom (Gender, Theology and Spirituality)* (London: Equinox, 2007), p. 258. See also <http://www. hildegard-society.org/2014/07/o-virtus-sapientie-antiphon.html>. Hildegard's composition can be heard on this site.

Holy Rood House and Wisdom

Holy Rood House, Centre for Health and Pastoral Care, is a charity in Thirsk, North Yorkshire, an earthy, creative, therapeutic and educational place offering space to those who need, for respite, healing, rest, and to breathe, in this chaotic world in which we live. We work on the margins of society, welcoming all, often guests who feel on the edge themselves, for short stay, day retreat and individual therapy. Some guests come to explore the transitions they are going through in their lives, and other guests come to engage with the theological work of the community. Justice, peace and ecology are important aspects of our workings. Hospitality is an integral part for all staff in the charity, as it is within hospitality that Wisdom can emerge. Some of our staff live on site—this is their home; other staff come in from their own homes. We have around 30 to 35 volunteers and paid staff contributing to the charity.

To give a flavour of what we offer at Holy Rood House and how we give opportunity for Wisdom to emerge, let us imagine that you would like to visit. Before you arrive, you arrange to come for a short stay or a day visit as, at some point, you have decided that it is right for you to have a retreat, some space to reflect, and perhaps some accompaniment with your present journey in life. Your decision may have come from your body-knowing, what you know you need. We all have to make decisions about what is best for ourselves in the different seasons of our lives, and we know how difficult it can be to arrange care for ourselves.

So you arrive, having discussed your requirements, what will suit you, and having an expectation of what will be offered. You are warmly welcomed into the community. Our welcome is important as we know that you will enhance our community in some way; we are not the experts, we are all in this place together. We recognize the way of Wisdom in the welcoming—we know you have this knowing within you and we welcome your knowing, even if this feels absent or chaotic to you.

We show you to your room. We try and make the house as safe a space as possible as we can only access our Wisdom with a sense of safety. So the private bedroom space is important. Guests who book for the day are also offered this bedroom space. Each bedroom has a small notebook where previous guests have written their encouragement and reflections. This links you to a flavour of the stories that are so important to our community, stories that connect us to the hope that we offer, which comes through the knowing we have. Your story will also add to this hope; your arrival is part of this story.

You will be given a programme for the week, a gentle structure of mealtimes, prayers and holistic offerings. Some guests would prefer more to be organized; however, as we leave you to arrange what is right for you within this structure it gives a chance for your Wisdom to come forth. The regular mealtimes, morning coffee and afternoon tea, help us to be nourished and to have meeting points within the day. Someone will always be around in these times, and we try and eat together as a community at lunch and dinner. Our food is homecooked and seasonal, linking us to the rhythms of the earth with some of the produce from our gardens.

At some point, the other spaces in the two houses and gardens will be shown to you. In Juliet House, there is a library and an art room for your use. These are key areas of the Centre for Study of Theology and Health—part of our charity that links with learning and education that helps us explore Wisdom. The library contains books on many subjects, including theology, counselling, psychology, pastoral care, ecology, creativity, spirituality and health. In the art room, there are many materials for play and exploration, the creative process being a way to open to our Wisdom. This house, along with the gardens and other spaces, may also be the focus of retreats held regularly throughout the year, and these spaces are also offered for hire for the many groups that appreciate our facilities.

The garden surrounds the two houses with plenty of reflective spaces to connect to our senses. Our quiet garden is an enclosed space housing a small chapel—Sophia's Chapel—for individual use. Our labyrinth offers a meditative focus and the pond a still place. Animals are an important part of our community, and you will be shown our current pets—perhaps goats, hens and a tortoise. They add to our inclusivity and our knowing that all creatures can be part of our learning and caring.

You may like to join us in our Chapel space, the walls held within our garden, where there is a regular rhythm of prayer. Here we connect to the earth and the seasons and hear from past saints and other Wisdom figures. Our prayerfulness incorporates our embodied beings where Wisdom happens. We link our community to the wider yearnings of the world, holding hope and listening to Wisdom's voice for all the injustices and demands. We trust the ritual of rhythm, of the various seasons, of our candle-lit offerings and the regular Eucharists, to bring healing, hope and change.

We have counsellors, psychotherapists and a chaplaincy team who offer one-to-one time to help your exploration. Holistic sessions may be offered that help us connect to our bodies, such as wellbeing, head massage, walks and meditation.

The two comfy lounges offer space to talk to other guests and staff if you would like. Someone from our chaplaincy team is around on many of the days you stay, for conversation and to keep a safe space. Laughter is often heard, as we know where there are sorrows there is often joy. We try not to give our issues power and to cloud who we are as individuals. We appreciate the small things of life, beauty and hope offered daily. We know we don't always get things right and that is acceptable. Your wish for a "successful" visit may not be to do with great change; it may be the start of finding a way forward, of discovering a different perspective, of appreciating what good food, the sensory gardens and love has enabled within you.

- www.holyroodhouse.org.uk
- www.facebook.com/holyroodhouse
- www.instagram.com/holy_rood_house

Ways of opening to Wisdom

Disciplines, creative ideas and information

There are suggestions throughout the book on ways to open to the way of Wisdom. The following ideas summarize and add to a few of these ways. They reflect the many different ways of opening to Wisdom; we are all unique and we need to explore what is right for us, and what suits the season we are going through. The addition of some useful websites and information may help further exploration.

Through the body

Deep breathing and observing the body

Connecting consciously to our breath is a key way of connecting to the body and opening the way of Wisdom. We can develop our breath so our in-breath travels down into our diaphragm, our abdomen, from our lungs, allowing for a deeper way of breathing in and breathing out from this deeper place. We can keep focused on our breath for a few minutes, releasing any intruding thoughts, helping us to root in the present moment.

For a calming breath, from this deeper breathing we can breathe in for a count of three and breathe out for a count of four.

There are many breathing exercises. One exercise is to imagine on the in-breath breathing down our front from head to feet, and on the out-breath breathing from the feet to the head. As we breathe in, we imagine the flow down our front, and as we breathe out, we imagine the flow up our back, so we have our breath form a circle around us. As we breathe in and out, we can imagine this circle gently expanding, to give us a protective energy breath circle around our bodies. This can add to the sense of spaciousness around us, formed from our imaginative breathing.

From our focus on our breathing, we can continue with observing our body:

- for tensions
- for our emotional states
- to observe our mind
- to open up to our senses—especially our touch, hearing and smell.

Imagining the spaciousness within
From the observing of the body, we can imagine the spaciousness within, our heart space. We can open up our inner eyes and ears to listen to our Wisdom from this spaciousness.

Finding ways to connect to all our senses
Connecting to our senses as we do our everyday tasks helps to bring us into the present moment and into the body. We can have times of enjoying our senses as we go out into nature or cook our dinner, for instance, trying out smelling, touching and hearing things we may not have noticed before.

Mindful walking
This is a lovely way to connect to the earth. We may like to have bare feet for this. We slowly plant the left foot as we breathe in and right foot as we breathe out, and as we move we become mindful of sensations and absorb the energy of the earth.

Healing hands
Using our hands to nurture parts of our body can connect us to our deep body-knowing. We can place our hands on areas of pain or tension, feeling the heat. We can anchor and calm our nervous system with self-holding, such as giving ourselves a hug, or holding one hand on our heart and one on our gut. We can gently press on various acupressure points on our body for release of energy. We can massage our feet with oil or

cream. We can use our hands for gestures, such as opening our hands, palms up, as a symbolic gesture of opening and listening to receive from our body-knowing.

For more information
The organization Capacitar International has many helpful exercises to connect to the body, the earth and our subtle energy. Capacitar means empowerment with the aim to awaken, to encourage, to bring each other to life.

- International and general link: www.capacitar.org
- UK link: www.capacitaruk.org

We teach body-based practices that empower people to use their inner wisdom to heal and transform themselves, to heal injustice and build peace in their families and communities.
There are helpful videos at www.capacitar.org/capacitar-videos.

Through noting our energy and finding our still point (in addition to Chapter 2).

We can note our energy at different times of the day, and what affects our energy. We may consider how thoughts, moods, feelings, relationships, exercise, food and drink, faith aspects and what we do in our everyday life affects our energy. What saps our energy? What increases our energy? Noticing our energy can help us to find where we feel balanced and connected to our true selves.

The balanced state and still point. This is where our energy seems to be flowing well, we feel more integrated, stable and balanced. We can feel calm and peaceful with a connection to joy. We can open to our "I am". This is a healing state.

Our energy may be too high. We may find our brain feels too stimulated, our emotions are high or overwhelming and we may have adrenaline coursing through our body. We may feel anxious and stressed, or too "buzzy". We may need some calming activities, such as noted above.

Our energy may be too low. Our energy seems to drag us down. We have low mood. Our thoughts are slow and we are unmotivated. We may need some gentle activities, such as walking, gardening, tai chi, massage, to help our energy flow.

We can find ways of noticing when this healthy point is tipped to make our mood or energy too low or too high, and explore how we right ourselves, or bring ourselves back to this still point. We can notice "What makes me feel like me?"; what resonates and connects to my purpose, motivation and gifts? This will be where our energy flows well.

The "window of tolerance" developed by psychiatrist Dan Siegel is a descriptive tool in noticing our balanced state. A diagram of this window shows a mid-area where our brain functions well and calmly and we feel grounded. Above this area is where we feel too stimulated and below is where our energy is low. In different seasons of our lives, the window of tolerance will be wider than others. Many people going through loss, trauma and grief find it difficult to understand why they cannot cope with tasks that they could do with ease in more comfortable times. These are times where our window of tolerance has narrowed. Our window of tolerance will widen as we nurture our energy and find the right support we need.[1]

Finding a rhythm of movement and rest/reflection

This rhythm can be helped by switching activities during the day. If we work on a computer for many hours, for instance, we may arrange breaks for physical connection, engaging with other senses, perhaps doing something creative with our hands or going for a walk. Setting up ways of rest and reflection can help balance our day. These allow times for us to listen and be open to our own Wisdom.

We may find a discipline for when we first awake—such as a body discipline, a time for meditation, or writing time that reminds us of the way of Wisdom. Similarly, towards the end of the day, we can have time for reflection, to listen to the small happenings, resonances and noticings that highlight Wisdom's process.

A Way of Reflection (based on The Examen by St Ignatius)
Sitting quietly, we connect to our breath.

We allow reflections of the day, noticing the little things that have occurred.

We open ourselves to what has caused a reaction—what has stirred our emotions, made us laugh, or tense, or hurt, for example. We notice what has brought joy, gratitude or peace, or maybe an increase or decrease in energy.

We sit with this in a quiet way with no judgement, just allowing this observing of the effects of what has happened.

We may like to take one thing from our reflections and stay with this. Just let it be held in our thoughts; perhaps held in love.

There are many apps, such as Insight Timer app, that have helpful meditations, breathing exercises, chanting and energy flow videos that can help with finding disciplines that suit us and link us in to our healing state.

Through creative ways, experimenting and exploring

We can enjoy the challenge of being the explorer, to find helpful disciplines to highlight the creative process where Wisdom emerges.

Journaling, using a flexible way of writing, drawing and experimenting, can be illuminating. There are many books to help with creative journaling; some are listed in the bibliography.

Poetry, art and music—slow looking and listening, reading, reflecting and composing all help us to note the creative process.

Play is important—either on our own or with others, especially with children who can teach us how to play.

Anything creative with our hands such as stitch, clay, painting, playing music, connects to our body-knowing and the creative process.

Using the imagination can help us to connect with mystery, such as imagining talking to our inner Wisdom.

Through nurture

By being kind and gentle with ourselves, we can develop a nurturing quality through our opening to Wisdom's way. We can find nurturing spaces, perhaps setting up a small area within our home for our reflection. It may be where some symbolic objects can be placed.

We can imagine nurturing images, such as the robe woven from every Wisdom offered in Chapter 6. We could use a blanket or shawl to put around us in our times of reflection.

Wisdom connects to love, and we can learn to be open to receive that love, however it comes to us.

Contemplation, stillness and prayer

We will all have our individual ways of listening to our Wisdom. For some people, coming into stillness through keeping the body quiet can be helpful. Techniques include meditation, mindfulness, centering prayer, focusing on a lit candle or something in nature, for example. It is finding ways to bypass the busy mind and drop down into our spaciousness.

One of the methods I use is that of active listening where I sit and open my inner ears to hear what is going on within me and around me. It is sitting being aware of, but not absorbed by, what is going on in my body, in my thoughts and my surroundings. This awareness is an alertness that is just noting where I am and what is going on, just listening to any promptings of the inner spirit.

For others, something more active can be helpful to open to our deeper spaciousness. Walking where we are present to our senses, for instance, or focusing on an activity with the hands, like colouring, gardening or craftwork.

Chanting, humming and singing can also be forms of contemplation. We can take lines from hymns or songs to sing, or to repeat a short phrase so that it sinks deeper into our spaciousness. We can also make up a simple tune, or sing on one note, taking a phrase from Wisdom literature, such as the Psalms, or perhaps a line from a poem. Humming can connect to these deep vibrational resonances within us.

We can find chants, such as Gregorian chant, ones from Hildegard and those connecting to nature, online. The Insight Timer app has helpful videos. I have started a quote book, where I note helpful phrases from various sources, and in one section I write them into a phrase that can work with a simple tune.

We can find imaginative ways of prayer such as imagining holding a situation or person in the light, or in a natural setting such as a garden. It is finding ways of prayer that open us to our own insights, rather than using others' insight, that is helpful for hearing our Wisdom.

Rituals such as lighting a candle, watching the sun going down in the afternoon or evening, connecting to seasons in nature and days in the church calendar can give us other considerations as we explore.

The Eucharist is a ritual that connects to the way of Wisdom. In Proverbs 9:5–6, Wisdom speaks:

> Come, eat of my bread and drink of the wine I have mixed. Lay
> aside immaturity and live, and walk in the way of insight.

From ancient times, the bread and wine has become a reminder of the presence of Wisdom within, that connects to the Divine "I am". Jesus used this ritual for a living remembrance of the connection and unity through the "I am", which he upheld and expressed.

Reading and reflecting on Wisdom literature

Lectio Divina is Latin for divine reading, and it is a way of reflection that opens us to Wisdom's process. A short passage is chosen—and this can be from Wisdom literature (mentioned in the bibliography), quotes from this book, or something that has resonated from a poem, a hymn or other source. Time is taken to settle and to savour perhaps one or two words, or a phrase, for focus. Through this focus, there may be emotions, memories and images that come up. We let them happen, although we might observe them, rather than letting them take over our thinking. We allow this focus to bring us into stillness. We may take something of this reading with us into the rest of the day, or night, for further openings.

Connecting to the earth

Going outside, getting into our senses, listening and sitting in nature, is valuable in our journeying. Using breathing exercises outside can give us a different experience than if we are inside. Many of the disciplines already noted can be taken into nature.

Observing wildlife and our pets when they are outside can help us to connect to the unity and belonging of all creatures. Guests enjoy watching our hens, scratching around and making their lovely clucking sounds. We are taken to different perspectives through the eyes of other creatures and experience their Wisdom of being in the now, doing what they need to do.

Lectio Divina can be experienced with natural beings at the centre of our reflecting. Either resting our eyes on something that catches our attention, or holding an object in our hand, we can spend time using our senses and imagination on what this natural being is saying to us. We can "be with" this being and allow that connection between us.

We can explore the different seasons, various weathers, the light and the dark, the earth and the sky. The natural world has a wealth of knowing to teach us.

We can hum and sing to the earth, speak to the river, dance on the grass, stretch with a tree, and enjoy the offerings received.

Finding community

Finding others, for exploration with Wisdom, and to help support us in our questings, can sometimes be tricky. It is finding people where we can be honest with our sharings and who may be willing to explore, perhaps creatively, perhaps with contemplation, reading or conversations, so together deeper aspects of life are discussed. The communities that we are drawn to may offer people with whom we can reflect. Perhaps this book can be a starter point for group exploration.

Knowing ourselves and our passions may lead us to groups where we can be more active with justice and peace issues and also find support.

Our voice and our story are important and need to be heard. This may be sharing with friends, getting to know our neighbours or speaking out in a group. There will be ways for us voicing what we are hearing from Wisdom's call.

Meeting with others for reflection, prayer and contemplation
There are many organizations that enable us to come together to open to Holy Wisdom. Here are a few:

- Julian meetings are set up around the UK for short times of contemplation. www.thejulianmeetings.net
- Quaker meetings: A Quaker meeting for worship creates a space of gathered stillness. In the quietness of the meeting, we can become aware of Wisdom's energy informing and uniting, transcending our ordinary, day-to-day experiences. All are welcome to the weekly Sunday meetings. www.quaker.org.uk/meetings
- WCCM (World Community of Christian Meditation) offer meditation groups and training days. www.wccm.org/meditate/meditation-groups
- The Retreat Association website links to various retreat houses, resources and events for us to find spaces for reflection. www.retreats.org.uk

Notes

1   <https://www.goodtherapy.org/blog/psychpedia/window-of-tolerance>.

APPENDIX 3

Dreams

Dreams are creative ways where Wisdom shines her light. The following is a brief outline for getting in touch with our dreams and there are some helpful books for more in-depth connection to our dreams listed in the bibliography.

Dreams are messengers helping us to understand our life, offering a perspective not able to be accessed in the reality of the everyday. We may experience nightmares that we prefer not to remember. Nightmares tend to build up over time when we are not listening to our inner Wisdom. There is always a healing element, a person or object that is showing us something, even if our dreams seem harsh. As the dream world is one of symbolism and imagination, we need to find ways of understanding.

We can start with intention. Many of us do not remember our dreams, however, once we start wanting to capture our dreams, we often start finding snippets. As we lie in bed with a glimpse of our dream, we can try and enlarge this, without distraction through moving or allowing other thoughts. Keeping the image in our minds can help bring it to life.

We can then write out this glimpse. If we have more, then we can choose whether to write out the larger part, or to focus on one small section. We write in the present tense. There may be an image that we draw out to help us remember. I had a dream of a tattoo on my elbow that I really wanted to capture. The shape led to an interesting creative activity.

Once written and/or drawn out, there are various techniques to help us to understand the dream language. The dreamwork technique in *Dreams and Spiritual Growth: A Judeo-Christian Way of Dreamwork*, recommended in the bibliography, starts by giving our dream a title, just something spontaneous that comes to us. It then suggests we state the theme—the major theme or issues which have surfaced in the dream.

Next the affect, our dominant feeling or emotional energy experienced in the dream. There may be more than one feeling and they may not be what we expect. Lastly the book suggests that we explore the question that the dream is asking of us. What is the dream trying to reveal?

We may want a special notebook that we leave by our bed to capture our dreams. Once we start noting dreams there are often interesting links between our dreams; symbols may appear again, or in another form, and we may recognize objects that crop up.

I also find Jung's outlook on dreams helpful—that each part of the dream is a part of myself. So all the people, objects and scenery are all parts of me. So speaking from that object or person in the dream can enlighten. For example, I can take the tattoo image and imagine what it might say if it had a voice. I can then take another object or character and do the same and then dialogue between the two parts.

We can also go back into our remembered dream and use our imagination to develop what might happen if the dream continued. If we have an upsetting dream, we may change the image and imagine a better image. We can often be empowered through our dreams as we start to understand them, and as we develop an outcome.

Being with my dreams develops more of an understanding within myself; they often sort, sift, heal, enlighten, settle and bring joy.

Bibliography

Wisdom literature

Old Testament: Proverbs, some of the Psalms, Job, Song of Songs and Ecclesiastes. The Apocrypha, especially Wisdom, Sirach (or Ecclesiasticus) and Baruch.

New Testament: Jesus teaches the way of Wisdom, so the Gospels are important in our exploration of Wisdom.

Other manuscripts mentioned are some of the texts uncovered from Nag Hammadi in Upper Egypt, including the Gospel of Thomas and *The Thunder, Perfect Mind:*

Patterson, Stephen J. and Robinson, James M. (trs), *The Gospel of Thomas*, adapted from Patterson, Stephen J., Robinson, James M. and Bethge, Hans-Gebhard, *The Fifth Gospel: The Gospel of Thomas Comes of Age* (Harrisburg, PA: Trinity Press International, 1998), pp. 7–32.
<https://www.biblicalarchaeology.org/daily/biblical-topics/bible-versions-and-translations/the-gospel-of-thomas-114-sayings-of-jesus/>
The Nag Hammadi Library—MacRae, George W. (tr.), *The Thunder, Perfect Mind,* <http://gnosis.org/naghamm/thunder.html>

Theological and spiritual

Barker, Margaret, *Temple Mysticism: An Introduction* (London: SPCK, 2011).
Bird, Catherine, *The Divine Heart of Darkness: Finding God in the Shadows* (Durham: Sacristy Press, 2017).

Bourgeault, Cynthia, *The Wisdom Way of Knowing: Reclaiming an Ancient Tradition to Awaken the Heart* (Hoboken, NJ: Jossey-Bass, 2003).

Bourgeault, Cynthia, *The Wisdom Jesus: Transforming Heart and Mind—A New Perspective on Christ and His Message* (Boston, MA: Shambhala, 2008).

Boyce-Tillman, June, *Unconventional Wisdom (Gender, Theology and Spirituality)* (London: Equinox, 2007).

Douglas-Klotz, Neil, *Desert Wisdom: A Nomad's Guide to Life's Big Questions from the Heart of the Native Middle East* (Worthington: ARC Books, 2011).

Fiorenza, Elisabeth Schüssler, *Wisdom Ways: Introducing Feminist Biblical Interpretation* (Maryknoll, NY: Orbis Books, 2001).

Fox, Matthew, *Meister Eckhart: A Mystic Warrior for our Times* (Novato, CA: New World Library, 2014).

Galland, China, *The Bond between Women: A Journey to Fierce Compassion* (New York: Riverhead Books, 1998).

Helminski, Kabir Edmund, *Living Presence (Revised): The Sufi Path to Mindfulness and the Essential Self* (New York: Tarcher Perigee, 2017).

Hildegard of Bingen, *Hildegard of Bingen's Scivias: Know the Ways*, tr. Bruce Hozeski (Sante Fe, CA: Bear & Company, 1986).

Hillesum, Etty, *An Interrupted Life: The Diaries, 1941–1943*, tr. Het Verstoorde Leven (New York: Pantheon Books, 1983).

Johnson, Elizabeth A., *She Who Is: The Mystery of God in Feminist Theological Discourse* (New York: The Crossroad Publishing Company, 1998).

Mother Julian of Norwich, *Revelations of Divine Love*, trs and eds Halcyon Backhouse and Rhona Pipe (London: Hodder & Stoughton, 1987).

Keller, Catherine, *On the Mystery: Discerning Divinity in Process* (Minneapolis, MN: Fortress Press, 2007).

Myss, Caroline, *Anatomy of the Spirit: The Seven Stages of Power and Healing* (London: Bantam, 1997).

Nouwen, Henri, *The Inner Voice of Love* (London: Darton, Longman & Todd, 1997).

Quaker Faith and Practice: the book of Christian discipline of the Yearly Meeting of the Religious Society of Friends (Quakers) in Britain, fifth edition (Oxford: Berforts Information Press, 2013). Online at <https://www.quaker.org.uk/resources/quaker-faith-and-practice>.

Smith, Cyprian, *The Way of Paradox: Spiritual Life as Taught by Meister Eckhart* (London: Darton, Longman & Todd, 1987).

Warwick, Helen, *The Life-Giving Path: Reflections for Personal Exploration and Discovery* (New Town Farm: Kevin Mayhew, 2016).

Wildwood, Alex, *A Faith to Call my Own* (London: Quaker Home Service, 1999).

Williams, Rowan, *Being Human: Bodies, Minds, Persons* (London: SPCK, 2018).

Woodhouse, Patrick, *Etty Hillesum: A Life Transformed* (London: Bloomsbury, 2009).

Psychological, therapeutic, scientific

Duff, Kat, *The Alchemy of Illness* (New York: Pantheon, 1993).

Ferrucci, Piero, *What We May Be: Techniques for Psychological and Spiritual Growth through Psychosynthesis* (New York: Tarcher/ Penguin, 2004).

Goleman, Daniel, *Emotional Intelligence: Why it can matter more than IQ* (London: Bantam Dell, 2005).

McKay, Matthew, Wood, Jeffrey, Brantley, Jeffrey, *The Dialectical Behavior Therapy Skills Workbook: Practical DBT Exercises for Learning Mindfulness, Interpersonal Effectiveness, Emotion Regulation and Distress Tolerance* (Oakland: New Harbinger, 2007). Based on the work of Dr Marsha Linehan.

Mindonca, Miguel, *Wisdom: Now and Always* (independently published, 2020).

Creativity, dreams

Cameron, Julia, *The Artist's Way* (London: Pan Macmillan, 1994).
Johnson, Robert A. (Jungian analyst), *Inner Work: Using Dreams & Active Imagination for Personal Growth* (San Francisco, CA: Harper San Francisco, 1991).
Klein, Doris, *Journey of the Soul* (Lanham, MD: Sheed & Ward, 2000).
Parker, Russ, *Healing Dreams: Their Power and Purpose in your Spiritual Life* (London: SPCK, 1993).
Savary, Louis, Berne, Patricia, Williams, Strephon Kaplan, *Dreams and Spiritual Growth: A Judeo-Christian Way of Dreamwork* (Mahwah, NJ: Paulist Press, 1984).
Valters Paintner, Christine, *The Artist's Rule: Nurturing Your Creative Soul with Monastic Wisdom* (South Bend, IN: Sorin Books, 2011).
Warwick, Helen, *Finding your Inner Treasure: A Spiritual Journey of Creative Exploration* (New Town Farm: Kevin Mayhew, 2010).

Ecological/spiritual

Blackie, Sharon, *The Enchanted Life: Reclaiming the Magic and Wisdom of the Natural World*, second edition (Tewkesbury: September Publishing, 2021).
Clinebell, Howard, *Ecotherapy: Healing Ourselves, Healing the Earth* (London: The Haworth Press, 1996).
Eisenstein, Charles, *The More Beautiful World Our Hearts Know Is Possible* (Berkeley, CA: North Atlantic Books, 2013).
Griffiths, Jay, *Wild: An Elemental Journey* (London: Penguin Books, 2008).
Macy, Joanna, *World as Lover, World as Self* (Berkeley, CA: Parallax Press, 1991).
McIntosh, Alistair, *Soil and Soul: People versus Corporate Power* (London: Aurum Press, an imprint of Quarto Publishing, 2004).

Poetry, liturgy and podcasts

Barks, Coleman, *Essential Rumi* (San Francisco: Harper San Francisco, 1995).

Barrows, Anita and Macy, Joanna (trs and eds), *A Year with Rilke: Daily Readings from the Best of Rainer Maria Rilke* (New York: HarperCollins, 2009).

Baxter, Elizabeth, *Holy Rood House Community Prayer* (independently published, 2017).

Baxter, Elizabeth (ed.), *Poetry and Art from Holy Rood House: A Celebration of 25 Years 1993–2018* (independently published, 2019).

Berry, Jan and Pratt, Andrew (eds) with Eldred, Janet and Sardeson, Anne, *Hymns of Hope and Healing: Words and Music to Refresh the Church's Ministry of Healing* (London: Stainer & Bell, 2017).

Bialock, Carol, *Coral Castles* (Portland, OR: Fernwood Press, 2019).

Eliot, T. S., *Four Quartets* (London: Faber & Faber, 1944).

Mitchell, Stephen (ed.), *The Enlightened Heart: An Anthology of Sacred Poetry* (New York: HarperCollins, 1994).

O'Donohue, John, *Benedictus: A Book of Blessings* (London: Bantam Press, 2007).

Rilke, Rainer Maria, *Rilke's Book of Hours: Love Poems to God*, Anita Barrows and Joanna Macy (trs and eds) (New York: Riverhead Books, 1997).

Ward, Tess, *Celtic Wheel of the Year: Celtic and Christian Seasonal Prayers* (Winchester: O Books, 2007).

Whyte, David, *River Flow: New and Selected Poems* (Langley, NJ: Many Rivers Press, 2012).

Wright, Revd Matthew, *Entering the bridal chamber of the heart.* Six sessions on YouTube from a three-day retreat exploring the Christian Wisdom tradition. Focusing on the Gospels of Thomas, Mary Magdalene, and Philip, <https://www.youtube.com/watch?v=2Yi4xsUIRqI>.

On-Being podcast, <https://onbeing.org/series/podcast/>.

Milton Keynes UK
Ingram Content Group UK Ltd.
UKHW020717300923
429690UK00012B/898